LIVING
INTENTIONALLY

How intentionality enables success, fulfillment, and growth

JOE GAGNON

INTENTIONAL LIVING PRESS
NEW YORK, NY

Cover and interior formatting by KUHN Design Group | kuhndesigngroup.com

Edited by: Robert Cheeke, Jordan Baskerville, and Grainne Daly

ISBN 979-8-9993011-1-6 (e-book)
ISBN 979-8-9993011-0-9 (TP)
ISBN 979-8-9993011-2-3 (HC)

First edition

PRAISE FOR *LIVING INTENTIONALLY*

"*Living Intentionally* provides a blueprint for a truly meaningful life. Equipped with innovative ideas for navigating modern challenges we're all faced with, Joe provides eloquent solutions with dynamic examples from his own inspiring journey."

—Dan Buettner, National Geographic Fellow and #1 *New York Times* Bestselling Author of *The Blue Zones*

"Thriving isn't about quick fixes or the pursuit of comfort. It's the growth that comes from embracing change, taking action, and nurturing resilience. This mindset not only transforms gut health but also fuels every aspect of our well-being. In *Living Intentionally*, you'll uncover how to tap into this limitless potential. Joe Gagnon exemplifies this philosophy—running ultramarathons around the world, pushing his limits with feats of strength, and embarking on ice-climbing adventures with his daughters. Let *Living Intentionally* inspire you to realize how truly expansive your potential is. Get the book and embark on your own journey toward a vibrant, empowered life."

—Dr. Will Bulsiewicz, *New York Times* Bestselling Author of *Fiber Fueled* and *The Fiber Fueled Cookbook*

"If there is one book you read this year, *Living Intentionally* should be it. Joe Gagnon shows us that when we align our actions with purpose, whether it's in how we eat, lead, move, or serve, we unlock something truly transformative. This is an inspiring guide for anyone ready to live with more clarity, energy, meaning, and joy."

—Carleigh Bodrug, *New York Times* Bestselling Author of *PlantYou* and *PlantYou: Scrappy Cooking*

"Joe Gagnon is the real deal. From his humble middle-class upbringing to becoming the CEO of six companies to running six marathons on six continents in six days, Joe's story is beyond impressive. Joe's journey is not only deeply inspiring but also very intentional. In *Living Intentionally*, Joe shares his secret formula with the rest of us, and after reading this book, you too will master the art of living."

—Rip Esselstyn, #1 *New York Times* Bestselling Author of *Plant-Strong*

"Joe Gagnon has been flying under the radar with his humble approach to intentional living, quietly setting an example for the rest of us to follow. That was, until now. *Living Intentionally* is poised to shake up the current narrative of personal transformation literature with a fresh take on what it means to live a life of purpose and leave a lasting legacy that will inspire generations to come. With this amazing new book, Joe will undoubtedly leave an indelible mark on readers and will transform lives for the betterment of society. Thank you, Joe."

—Dotsie Bausch, Olympic Silver Medal-Winning Cyclist and Founder of Switch4Good

"I've worked directly with Joe Gagnon, and I was immediately impressed with his wisdom, experience, and unique ability to inspire others. He sets a pragmatic and positive example for all team members, and it motivates everyone to rise up. In *Living Intentionally*, you can't hide from Joe's thoughtfulness and attention to detail. After reading this book, you'll be equipped to be a physical and intellectual champion. I highly recommend reading this book—your future self is waiting."

—Cyrus Khambatta, PhD, *New York Times* Bestselling Coauthor of *Mastering Diabetes*

"Joe Gagnon's *Living Intentionally* is a rare blend of emotional honesty, tactical self-development, and vision-oriented clarity. It reads like a mix of David Goggins's rawness, Simon Sinek's pursuit of purpose, and a bit of Ryan Holiday's philosophical framing—but without trying to be any of them. It's distinctly Joe, and that authenticity, combined with a next level of pure badass, is one of its greatest assets."

—Matthew de Gruyter, Cofounder and CEO of Next Level Burger

"In *Living Intentionally*, Joe Gagnon teaches us to aim higher than we ever believed possible, not to flatter our ego, but to unveil and unleash the highest and best version of ourselves. In doing so, Joe inspires us to be truly of service to the world, raising the level of consciousness and success for our communities as we do so for ourselves. This is how we can progress as a society in a way that everyone feels connected and valued, contributing with purpose and a desire for a brighter future for all. Thank you, Joe, for this timely addition to my home library."

—Ravi Raman, Executive Coach and Entrepreneur

"*Living Intentionally* nails what every endurance athlete and dreamer understands deep down: the magic isn't in comfort; it's in pushing through the hardest moments when everything says stop. Joe Gagnon captures that reality with clarity and conviction. This is a book for anyone who knows that real growth lives just beyond what feels possible."

—Pete Kostelnick, Record-Setting Ultramarathon Runner and Trans-America Record Holder

"As an entrepreneur and cyclist, I know that pushing limits isn't glamorous; it's gritty, demanding, and often uncomfortable. In *Living Intentionally*, Joe Gagnon brings that truth to life with clarity and inspiration. This book is a powerful guide for anyone who knows that progress, whether in life, on the saddle, or in building a business, comes from embracing challenge, staying present, and showing up day after day with purpose."

—Matt Lyon, Founder and CEO of HydraPak

"There are rare individuals who come into our lives and, simply by being who they are, lift us up, shift our mindset, and illuminate our path forward. Joe Gagnon is one of those people for me. Joe doesn't just talk about living with purpose—he embodies it, runs with it (literally), and generously shares the wisdom he's earned from a life lived on the edge of what's possible in his latest book, *Living Intentionally*. This book is a touchstone for anyone craving alignment with their personal *why*. It's fuel for your next bold step, and a soulful reminder that an extraordinary life isn't something you stumble into—it's something you choose, moment by intentional moment. *Living Intentionally* isn't just a read—it's a revelation. A blueprint. A battery pack for the soul. If you want to not just dream about a better life but live it, run, don't walk, to get your copy."

—Dr. Kelly Sullivan Walden, Bestselling Author of *Dreamifesting*

"When I think about the trajectory of my career, from my first job out of college under Joe's mentorship to now leading a multibillion-dollar business, one thread runs through it all: how we choose to show up is everything. Joe was the first to instill this idea in me. Intentions matter. They are the force behind our success, guiding how we lead, how we connect, and how we navigate the inevitable challenges of life and business. Living intentionally is an early lesson that has guided me more than I realized. Through Joe's words and experiences, you'll discover what I learned firsthand: success isn't accidental. It's a daily, deliberate act of bringing your whole self to every moment. This book will help you do just that."

—Suzanne Dann, CEO of Wipro Americas

"*Living Intentionally* is a powerful reminder that real transformation doesn't come from hacks or hustle—it comes from aligning your actions with your purpose and an unwavering commitment to growth. Joe Gagnon doesn't just talk the talk—he lives it. His story is raw, real, and a wake-up call for anyone ready to stop drifting and start *choosing* how they live. This book is for anyone ready to reclaim their power, challenge their limits, and show up fully for their life."

—Ella Magers, MSW, Holistic Fitness
Coach, Author, Host, and Founder

"From the moment I met Joe Gagnon, I knew he was built differently—not just physically, but mentally. His mindset, forged through tackling some of life's hardest challenges, is nothing short of inspiring. Joe is a mentor, role model, and keynote speaker who lights up every stage and moves people to push beyond their limits. He helped me complete my first ultramarathon—proof that he doesn't just talk the talk, he walks (and runs) it. In

Living Intentionally, Joe gives us more than motivation—he offers a roadmap to our highest potential, grounded in his own remarkable path of self-discovery, grit, and growth. This book is powerful. Read it, live it, and get ready to change your life."

—**David Atkins, Motivational Keynote Speaker, Author of** *The One Decision Away Philosophy*, **and Retired New York State Police Captain.**

"Joe Gagnon gets what it means to push limits—not just physically, but mentally, emotionally, and intentionally. In *Living Intentionally*, he shares a lifetime of endurance, leadership, and inner work, offering a roadmap for those who want to grow with purpose and heart. As someone who has raced across the world's most rugged terrain, from the Sahara Desert to the Himalayas, I resonated deeply with Joe's reflections on challenge, resilience, and what it means to live with intention. His work echoes the same values I spoke about on the TEDx stage: curiosity, consistency, and gratitude. This book is an invitation to reimagine what's possible—and a call to move forward with courage, clarity, and joy."

—**Sonya Looney, World Champion Mountain Biker, Positive Psychology Expert, TEDx Speaker, Mental Performance Coach, and Host of** *Grow the Good* **Podcast**

"Joe Gagnon doesn't just write about high performance and resilience—he lives it. His journey is extraordinary, and in this book, he offers practical, hard-earned wisdom that will resonate with anyone striving to align their actions with their values. An energizing and uplifting read."

—**Dr. Alan Desmond, Gastroenterologist, Author of** *The Plant-Based Diet Revolution*, **and Host of** *The Eat This Podcast*

"*Living Intentionally* is a reminder that greatness doesn't come from talent alone, it comes from conscious choices made every day. Joe Gagnon understands that the real endurance challenge is life itself. His words echo what I've learned on the trails and in the classroom: that discipline, purpose, and a clear *why* are the true drivers of performance. As a fellow plant-based ultrarunner, I see in Joe's story a reflection of the power that comes from living in alignment with your values, your health, and your dreams. This book is fuel for anyone who wants to go farther in running, in life, and in purpose."

—Harvey Lewis, World-Class Ultrarunner, Plant-Based Athlete, and Educator

"As someone who's experienced firsthand the power of lifestyle change—from struggling with asthma and weight management as a child and into my teens to reclaiming my health with the aid of plant-based nutrition—I deeply connect with the message of *Living Intentionally*. Joe's words resonate with the work I do every day in my clinical practice with the aim of empowering people to make lifestyle changes that support their long-term health. *Living Intentionally* is a guide for anyone ready to step into the driver's seat of their life and take action."

—Dr. Matthew Nagra, Doctor of Naturopathic Medicine

"*Living Intentionally* hit me in a place deeper than intellect; it spoke to legacy, to purpose, and to the responsibility we each carry to break cycles and build something better. I've seen too many lives cut short, including those closest to me, because of preventable, lifestyle-driven diseases. I am on a mission to shift the narrative in communities most impacted by health disparities. Joe's book is a timely and necessary companion in that mission. It challenges us to stop drifting and start designing lives of meaning, health, and service. This isn't a book of theory—it's a call to action. And for anyone ready to rise, *Living Intentionally* offers the clarity, courage, and conviction to do just that."

—Dr. Columbus Batiste, the Healthy Heart Doc, Double Board-Certified Cardiologist, and Author of *Selfish*

"*Living Intentionally* isn't just a book—it's a wake-up call to tune into what lights you up and start living with real purpose. Joe walks the talk, achieving incredible athletic feats (all fueled by plants), and in a world built for comfort and convenience, he reminds us that the discomfort zone is where true growth lives. The main kicker: his message that lasting change starts with your *why*. That's what fueled my own shift to a plant-based lifestyle. Taking baby steps and making choices that aligned with that *why* is how transformations happen.

Joe's stories are deeply inspiring for anyone feeling stuck or ready for something more. His five pillars—exercise, nutrition, sleep, mindset, and connection—offer a solid foundation for living with intention and meaning. This book is a powerful reminder that challenge fuels growth, that discipline can be liberating, and that when we live intentionally, we show up better for ourselves, our communities, and the planet. If you're ready for your next chapter to feel aligned, energized, and full of purpose, this book is your inspirational starting point."

—Julia Murray, a.k.a. @hookedonplants, Olympian, Plant-Based Nutritionist/Chef, and Do-Good Whistler Realtor

"Living Intentionally is a masterclass in reclaiming agency over your life, body, mind, and purpose. Joe Gagnon's insights echo the very principle that changed my life personally and the lives of so many patients in my medical practice: growth doesn't happen by chance; it's the product of conscious choices, often made in the face of challenge. Our greatest breakthroughs happen when we stop masking symptoms and start addressing the root of who we are and how we live. This book is a blueprint for living with clarity and conviction. It reminds us that just as we can transform our health by changing what we put on our plate, we can transform our lives by changing how we show up in the world."

—Dr. James F. Loomis, Medical Director at Barnard Medical Center, Cohost of *The Doc and Chef,* and Featured in the Documentary *The Game Changers*

"Living Intentionally is a powerful reminder that high performance isn't just for a select few; it's for anyone willing to make bold, aligned choices every day. Joe Gagnon brings the grit of an ultrarunner, the heart of a coach, and the wisdom of lived experience into every page. His message, that we're all capable of far more than we think, echoes what I've seen firsthand through plant-based endurance: when you fuel your body and your life with intention, you unlock new levels of energy, clarity, and purpose. This book is an inspiring call to go further, in running and in life."

—Matt Frazier, *New York Times* Bestselling Coauthor of *The Plant-Based Athlete* and Ultramarathoner

For those who dare to dream, who choose
purpose over comfort, and who live each
day with intention—this is for you.

Through quiet courage and meaningful action, a path is
lit for others to follow toward growth, reflection, and the
belief that more is possible when we live with intention.

CONTENTS

FOREWORD

E very so often, if you are lucky, you come across someone who makes an immediate impact on your life and alters your life's trajectory for the better. I am one of the fortunate ones because that's precisely what happened to me when I met Joe Gagnon. It was during a particularly challenging transition when I was between jobs, questioning my self-worth, and wondering how to best contribute to the world around me when our paths crossed. Truth be told, I was initially intimidated by Joe's accomplishments when we collaborated on a project together, but that feeling quickly faded when I witnessed Joe's passion for serving others and his desire for everyone around him to succeed, too. Working with Joe prompted me to reflect on my own vision of a life well-lived, inspiring me to reevaluate my talents and how to best use them for good.

In *Living Intentionally*, Joe creates a blueprint to follow to live our best lives, complete with stories of those who are squeezing the most out of life. It's not just a pursuit of happiness that we're all chasing, but it's a quest to find deeper meaning in our actions that will make the world a better place. It starts with asking ourselves the all-important question, "Why?" What's the *why* behind our goals, dreams, and aspirations that fuels our own purpose-driven life? Once we establish our *why*, we will be well on our way toward achieving the foundation of living an intentional life. And at the end, we create a legacy we leave behind that reflects the purpose and drive we put behind our *why*. Between our *why* and our legacy lie many stepping stones—each taking us another step closer to our desired destination and often rooted in happiness, fulfillment, and inspiration passed along to others.

I can say with confidence that Joe is one of the highest achievers I've ever met, and I can also say without reservation that Joe is one of the most purpose-driven, hardest-working, and consistently optimistic individuals that I have been fortunate to spend time with. What Joe taught me is that if we live intentionally, we set ourselves up for success, but we also bring more meaning to our lives, which in turn provides more clarity, happiness, joy, and fulfillment. He also taught me a lot about reframing one's perspective and language around failures, and how to see them as growth and learning opportunities. Joe encouraged me to slow down, to be present, and to acknowledge that we're only living in this very moment, right now. The desire or temptation to look over our shoulder at yesterday's troubles, or glance over the crest of tomorrow's worries, only robs us of the joy to be experienced right now, in this present moment. We need to simply *be*. To be still, to be aware, to be tuned in and engaged with our surroundings, and to appreciate the beauty that is all around us.

Living Intentionally is truly an enjoyable reading experience, filled with life-changing principles to incorporate into your own life. Joe's carefully curated lexicon is not only inspirational to me as a fellow author, but it's also intentional. One of the powerful messages in the book is the importance of choosing our words with care and clarity, as the language we use shapes our perspective and supports our growth. These practices involve replacing negative words, adopting empowering language, practicing daily affirmations, and modeling reframing language for others, among myriad other techniques to improve our communication, even with ourselves. Quite simply, it makes this book that much more enjoyable to read and to get fully immersed in while you're taken on an empowering path of self-discovery and intentionality. Joe reminds us that our words are seeds, and what we say plants the mindset we live by. When we speak with intention, we create a mental environment where possibility can take root and thrive.

What I greatly appreciate about Joe's approach to *Living Intentionally* is his evident lack of ego, despite his never-ending list of accomplishments as both an athlete and a business CEO. It speaks volumes about Joe's character, and as a reader, it's also a breath of fresh air in a genre where many "self-help" authors lead with self-regard. Joe left his ego at the door when he showed up with the intention to write this book because this book is for you, not for him. Furthermore, the tone Joe sets is one of optimism, hope, and aspiration during a time of great uncertainty. Joe's mindset that every day "is a vacation day" keeps him optimistic even in the face of challenges. That's something we can all learn from.

It's worth taking a moment to reflect on Joe's impact on me. I was the first person to read *Living Intentionally* from start to finish, and I was moved by the stories he shared and inspired by the quality and uniqueness of this book. Most importantly, this book has had a real impact on my life. Joe's message has helped me manage rejection, failure, and difficult situations more effectively. It has enhanced my awareness of and determination towards the goals I strive to achieve. Perhaps the most notable influence *Living Intentionally* has had on me is my increased ability to say "no" to the small things so that I can say "yes" to the big, important things. Additionally, Joe's book has helped me realize my own hidden potential, leading to business opportunities I never thought I'd experience. Gaining the confidence to fully invest in the things that truly enrich my life has been a very welcome addition to my own life well-lived. I am grateful for the opportunity to read an advanced copy and apply what I've learned from *Living Intentionally*.

My wish for you is that you glean as much wisdom from this book as I have and that you pursue your own meaningful ambitions with greater confidence and resolve, knowing that your intentionality is part of a winning formula in a purpose-driven life. As Joe reminds us: your endless journey starts now. What legacy will you leave behind? Take action and make your dreams happen. Your intentional life begins now.

—**Robert Cheeke,**
New York Times bestselling coauthor
of *The Plant-Based Athlete*

LIVING INTENTIONALLY IN A WORLD OF ACCELERATION

Throughout history, we've lived through inflection points—moments when innovation didn't just change how we live but how we understand ourselves. The printing press democratized knowledge. The Industrial Revolution redefined labor. The internet shrank the world. Each era brought tremendous opportunity, and an unspoken test: not whether we could adapt but whether we could do so without losing what makes us human.

Today's transformation is different. It's not just the scale; it's the speed. Technology, especially artificial intelligence, is advancing so quickly that it's outpacing our habits, our institutions, and even our ability to process what's happening. Nearly everything we interact with is being optimized to remove friction with recommendations for what to watch, where to eat, who to date, and what to buy. Our phones finish our sentences, our apps predict our preferences, and our feeds are fine-tuned to hold our attention.

It all works beautifully.

Well, sort of. As the technology around us grows more intelligent, we risk becoming less intentional. When every choice is made easier, we stop noticing that we're even making them. The systems anticipate what we want before we know it ourselves, and in that seamlessness, something vital slips away. In the comfort of convenience, we begin to surrender the one thing that defines us: our agency.

I experienced this firsthand on a recent trip to Phoenix. Instead of booking an Uber, I opened the Waymo app, an autonomous vehicle service, a.k.a. a driverless car. Ten minutes later, I was gliding through the city in a Waymo, with no one at the wheel! The ride was flawless. Smooth. Impressive. But oddly disorienting. Everything worked exactly as it should. The car knew where to go. But did I? That moment became more than a marvel of technology; it became a metaphor. Because the real threat of this age isn't that machines will overtake us. It's that the comfort of convenience can numb our desire to explore. The certainty of optimization can dull our capacity for wonder. And the promise of ease can quietly erode our pursuit of meaning.

This is where *Living Intentionally* begins.

It's a call to presence, to live not by default but by design. In a world designed to distract and automate, this book serves as a guide to finding meaning, intention, and what truly matters to each of us. At the center is a framework I've lived, tested, and taught: Grit, Grace, and Groundedness. These three pillars are more than ideas; they're the foundation of intentional living. They're daily disciplines that keep us anchored, aligned, and present amid the noise.

- Grit is our refusal to trade growth for comfort. It's how we keep going when everything says stop. Not loud or heroic, but the quiet strength to lean into hard things and keep moving forward.

- Grace is the power of compassion for others, yes, but especially for ourselves. It's how we forgive the stumble, begin again, and rise without shame. Without grace, grit turns into punishment. With grace, progress becomes sustainable.

- Groundedness is presence with depth. It's knowing what we stand for and staying rooted there. In a world filled with noise and novelty, groundedness is a radical act of remembering who we are.

These pillars are not personality traits; they're practices, ways of showing up, especially when it's difficult. They help us resist the drift toward passivity and reclaim the power that only intentional living can offer. This book isn't about technology, but it exists within the tension of this moment, an age of acceleration, abundance, and the quiet erosion of human depth. Thus, the choice becomes urgent: "Will we let life happen to us or will we choose to shape it?" This book is your companion in that pursuit. It offers stories, tools, frameworks, and challenges; more than anything, it's an invitation to hold onto your agency, connect with what matters, and live each day in a way that not only shapes your life but also defines who you are becoming.

**In a world speeding forward, living
intentionally is the quiet revolution.**

**To be fully present. Fiercely intentional.
Unapologetically human.**

INTRODUCTION

I couldn't sleep....

The Sydney hotel room was quiet except for the soft hum of the air conditioner, but my mind wouldn't stop racing. In just a few hours, I'd begin a challenge that sounded almost absurd: six marathons on six continents in six days. The anticipation pulsed through me—not just nerves, but a deep awareness that this wasn't just about running. This was about answering a question that had echoed in me for years: *What am I truly capable of when I remove the limits I place on myself?*

I wasn't doing this for records or headlines. This was personal. A quest to stretch my physical, emotional, and mental boundaries; to see if I could operate at the edge of human potential and emerge transformed. I had meticulously prepared for and visualized the miles, the exhaustion, the jet lag, the pain. But lying there in the dark, I knew no amount of training could simulate what lay ahead. I stared at the note I had written and taped to my suitcase: "The lows will be the highs." Simple words for an insane challenge. A mantra for the discomfort to come. Eventually, sleep came, and with it, a new dawn and the sun peeking through the curtains.

Morning arrived with that surreal quality that big moments often have. I stuck to my routine: a cup of black coffee, a PB&J sandwich, and light stretching. My bag sat packed, ready for the adventure ahead. I would be leaving Australia immediately after the first marathon, then making four stops (Singapore, Johannesburg, London, São Paulo) before finally landing in Los Angeles. Here we go. It all felt dreamlike.

I always knew I wanted to start this adventure in Australia. Not just because I had friends there, but because beginning something massive requires a foundation of trust. My friend, Kristen, promised to handle everything, telling me that all I had to do was run. When I arrived at the Sydney Harbour Bridge, Kristen and the crew were already there, waiting. And that's when it hit me. This wasn't just another run; it was the culmination of a year of planning and a lifetime of pushing my limits. The plan was simple: run 26.2 miles, the marathon distance, six days in a row, traversing each local landscape. These were not sanctioned marathons, making each run unique and of my choosing. It all translated into me spending twelve hours in each country, then twelve hours flying overnight to the next continent, then "wash, rinse, repeat." A nearby car horn snapped me back to reality. The sky was impossibly blue. There was a bit of small talk, and before I knew it, I was on my way to completing marathon number one. The rhythm of the challenge took over. Crossing the bridge, I reminded myself why I was doing this. Not for headlines or medals, but to explore the outer edges of human potential. The miles clipped along smoothly. I couldn't have chosen a better place to begin. The stunning Sydney skyline became a backdrop to the rhythm of my feet, and I soaked in every moment as I made my way to Centennial Park, where I ran four laps with Luke, one of my best mates from

Melbourne, riding alongside me on his bike. Our conversation made the miles disappear, and before I knew it, I was on the final stretch, finishing on the steps of the iconic Sydney Opera House.

I felt strong, and I had achieved my goal: finishing in under four hours. A few quick photos, a brief TV interview, and then Kristen's urgent reminder: "Time for the airport." There was no time to celebrate, no time to rest. This was all happening. I was living my belief that real growth comes when we intentionally push beyond comfort, beyond limits, into the unknown. One marathon down. Five more to go.

What followed was a lesson in human endurance, and each marathon had its own unique challenge. Singapore, my next stop, was without a doubt the toughest. I started at five a.m. to avoid the heat, and yet, the temperature was already a staggering ninety degrees, with humidity an unbearable 90 percent. A friend of mine, Richard, was my entire support crew, and, well, let's just say things didn't go exactly as planned. At mile seven, parched and struggling in the heat, I reached out for a drink.

"Drink?" Richard mumbled, confused.

"Yeah, the Gatorade," I replied with a sense of urgency.

"Oh...I left it in the car," he admitted.

I nearly lost it. Here I was, drenched in sweat, running in oppressive conditions with nothing to drink. But what choice did I have? Stopping wasn't an option, so I kept going. By mile fifteen, Richard had finally found some fluids, but the damage was done. I was drained. The next eleven miles were some of the hardest I had ever run. Yet, somehow, I finished in under four hours, and just like that, we were off to the airport.

Landing in Johannesburg (locals call it Joburg) at six a.m., I was given a VIP arrival treatment usually reserved for foreign dignitaries.

I was feeling quite special in Joburg; they rarely had someone like me come to do this kind of adventure. As my driver whisked me to my first stop, a local high school, for a photo opportunity and a presentation, he told me all about living in South Africa. He was so curious about why I had selected Joburg for my run, and we talked about the energy of the youth movement across the country. It was truly rewarding to talk to the room full of kids about the power of pushing beyond limits and how they could do the same in their lives. I was reminded again about the impact that we can make by choosing to lean into big challenges and share our dreams out loud with others. A few TV and radio interviews later, it was time to run.

The altitude of six thousand feet above sea level added a whole new layer of difficulty, but the energy of the local runners, about fifty of them who joined me, kept me moving. What happened over those few hours was more than just another run—it was connection, community, and something sacred in motion. These moments pass quickly on the clock but leave something permanent in the heart. We couldn't stop hugging and high-fiving at the finish line, the feeling of exhilaration shared among a group of strangers who, for a few unforgettable hours, became family. That was indeed something else. Another sub-four-hour finish—with three marathons completed and three still to go.

The flight to London felt endless. Exhausted and running on just a few hours of sleep, the reality of my coach-seat challenge was setting in. But there was no time for self-pity. My UK friends were waiting at the airport, ready to drive me straight to Windsor Castle, a breathtaking backdrop for another 26.2 miles. I felt at home in London. Having visited there more than twenty-five times, it was comforting to be in familiar territory. But as familiar as it was, somewhere along the course, I took a wrong turn, unintentionally adding distance to the run. It was frustrating, and I did my best to keep putting one foot in front of the other. As I kept pushing, I kept telling myself: "Only two more marathons to go." But that did not seem to make it any easier. Regardless, and to my relief, time continued to pass. I accepted the discomfort and pushed on to lock in another sub-four-hour finish. Four done, two to go, and another long flight ahead. Heathrow, here we come!

Next stop: São Paulo, Brazil. A grueling thirteen-hour flight, stuck in the middle seat, left me even more drained. The intriguing part of these multi-day challenges is the power of our intention. I was setting out to find the edges of human potential, and each stop reinforced and validated my purpose. From my years of pushing myself, running thousands of miles, and being part of other extreme challenges, I learned that an intention goes deeper than an idea; it is the embodiment of commitment to a goal and action. It is an explicit representation of who we are and how we show up. I leaned on my intention deeply on the flight to São Paulo, and it made a difference. When I arrived, something shifted. I felt a surge of energy; the discomfort was becoming the vehicle to achievement. I was rising to the occasion and felt the incredible responsibility of the challenge that I had taken on. So many people were connecting their hopes for what is possible to what I was doing. This was no longer about me; it was about all of us. If you have ever been to São Paulo, you would know that it is one of the busiest, most traffic-laden cities in the world. So, I was shocked when I arrived and saw the streets quiet due to the Good Friday holiday. *Oh wow, this is really different,* I thought to myself. Maybe it was the lack of other sporting events going on, but the ESPN of Brazil greeted me and followed my entire run, which they showed on TV across the country that evening! As it turns out, millions of Brazilians witnessed my run! Who would have known? Yet again, it showed how the world responds when we lean into it. The three city parks we ran through were the perfect setting to share my experience with a large group of friends who spent the day with me. Their energy fueled me, and against all odds, I ran my fastest marathon of the challenge. Five down, one to go.

When I landed in Los Angeles and went through US Customs and Immigration, I thought, *oh my gosh, I am home.* It was a surreal feeling; more than thirty thousand miles of flying around the globe, having not laid down for five days, and here I was in the LA International terminal, wondering, *how did I get here?* I was overcome by the awesome sensation of what was to be the final 26.2 miles. When I started this challenge, there was no guarantee that I would make it back to America in six days from the other side of the world. I had purposefully blocked out all the potential issues that could have arisen, and interestingly, none of them happened, or maybe I just didn't notice. Maybe that note to self, "the lows will be the highs," framed it all. Could it be that our mindset is the context setter for our journey and that everything else in our lives fits into it, not the other way around? Could it be that setting an intention makes a difference and takes us to the next level? I was living it, experiencing it, and feeling it, and I was practically shaking with the flow of energy bubbling inside of me. I made my last airport bathroom stop, brushed my teeth, changed into my running gear, washed up, and got ready to finish this challenge.

The crew who met me on the Redondo Beach Pier to send me off on the last 26.2 miles was buzzing, music was blaring, friends were chanting, "Run, Joe, run!" and I was launched north, running on the Strand along the Pacific Ocean. Could it be more iconic than running through Manhattan Beach, Marina del Rey, and Venice Beach? Sure, my legs were heavy, and I could feel the 150 miles or so of running, but with ten miles to go, it hit me: the months of preparation, the sleepless flights, the grueling miles, the discomfort, the incredible people who had supported me, all of it had led to this moment. We have all felt emotional at some point in our lives, but this feeling was unlike anything I had ever felt. Time had evaporated, I was completely absorbed in the moment, I had an intense level of focus, and I could feel my body vibrating; my mind was in a hyperstate of consciousness, and I effectively floated my way to the finish. I found what I went to find, and wow, did I feel it.

As I crossed the "finish line" in Santa Monica at the New Roads School, I was met with cheers, flashing cameras, and a flood of questions. But what truly struck me wasn't the media attention or the accomplishment itself. It crystallized into a single insight: living intentionally isn't about the destination. It's about choosing to push beyond comfort, beyond limits, into the unknown. It's about proving what's possible, not just for me, but for anyone willing to dream big and push beyond their supposed limits. Because I have found again and again that we *can* do more than we think we can.

WHAT THIS BOOK IS ABOUT

We all face our own marathons in life. Maybe it's launching a business, committing to a radical health transformation, or simply choosing to be more present in our daily lives. The challenge itself doesn't matter. What matters is the choice to live with intention. Whatever it is, the principle remains the same: we become the architects of our lives when we start making decisions with intention.

We are all given a finite amount of time, yet how we choose to use it makes all the difference. Some people drift through life, reacting to circumstances and letting the currents of routine pull them along. Others—those who leave an indelible mark, who achieve their greatest potential—live with intention. They take control of their days, align their actions with their values, push beyond comfort, and create lives of purpose and fulfillment. This book is about the latter path, the path of intentional living. It's about recognizing that every choice we make, every habit we form, and every challenge we embrace shape not just our present but our entire future. *Living Intentionally* is not about grand gestures or radical overnight change; it's about small, conscious, and deliberate actions that, over time, create extraordinary results.

WHAT YOU CAN EXPECT

Throughout this book, we'll explore the principles that fuel an intentional life. You'll read stories of people who pushed themselves beyond what they thought possible. Individuals who, like you and me, weren't born superhuman but chose to show up with awareness, purpose, and persistence.

In Chapter 3, you'll meet Diana Nyad, whose mantra "find a way" helped her become the first person, after four failed attempts, to swim from Cuba to Florida at age sixty-four. In Chapter 5, we'll explore how to turn failure into fuel. In Chapter 7, we'll step into the Tahoe 200, an ultra-race that cracked me open in ways I never expected. In Chapter 9, we'll explore how to connect our goals to something greater than ourselves. But this book isn't just about stories, it's about action. You'll find frameworks and exercises that help you integrate each principle into your own life. Whether it's refining your daily routines, deepening your mindset, or navigating discomfort, you'll come away with tools to build a life of intention from the inside out.

As you dig into each chapter, you'll notice it begins with a short reflection—a piece of writing pulled from my daily blog, *The High Performance Life*. These were not written with a book in mind, but they've become the foundation for how I live and lead intentionally. Over the years, thousands of these posts have captured moments of clarity, challenge, and insight. I've chosen one to open each chapter because it sets the tone. It's a way to ground the theme that follows in something real, personal, and lived. Consider these openings as mindset markers—brief pauses to frame what's to come and invite you to step into the chapter with curiosity and purpose.

THE CHOICE IS YOURS

Living intentionally is not about perfection. It's about ownership. It's about waking up each day and deciding consciously, deliberately that you will not simply exist, but that you will *live* with purpose. As you read through this book, I encourage you to reflect on your own life. What do you want to achieve? Where are you holding yourself back? And most importantly, what will you do about it? This book is about what your journey can become. It's about the habits, mindset shifts, and actions that separate those who drift through life lost in habitual, comfortable patterns from those who design it. It's about challenging yourself to push beyond what's easy and familiar, embracing the unknown, and stepping into the fullness of who you can be.

If you've ever felt the whisper that there's more for you—more to experience, achieve, or become—this book is your manual. It serves as both a guide and a challenge. A guide to help you build a life fueled by awareness, purpose, and discipline, and a challenge to break through self-imposed limits and embrace discomfort, which is where real growth happens. This book is your invitation.

Step forward. Take control.

Build the life you were meant to live.

Let's begin.

CHAPTER 1

DEFINING OUR *WHY*

Brick by Brick

There's something timeless about our desire to build a life that matters. It lives deep in our bones—a quiet longing to shape something lasting from the raw material of our days. When we look at those who came before us, we see that their greatness didn't arrive all at once. It was crafted slowly and patiently. Brick by brick. A habit formed. A challenge met. A connection nurtured. These moments, often ordinary in their passing, begin to reveal a larger design. And when that design is rooted in purpose, the ordinary transforms. The bricks become sacred. They form the foundation, not just of a life, but of a legacy. Sometimes, we forget why we are building. We lay bricks because we're told to, because the world moves fast, and because it's easier to keep going than to stop and wonder. But purpose invites us to pause. It offers a blueprint, and the pieces come together to make sense and form our foundation. Even the smallest act becomes an act of intention. Not

1

just motion but meaning. Not just a wall but our cathedral. "Brick by brick" reminds us: the extraordinary isn't waiting at the finish line. It's here, in the quiet placing of one stone upon another, guided by something deeper than ambition—something we carry within.

LIVING INTENTIONALLY

I had the corner office. The big paycheck. The respect of my peers. The American Dream, served with a side of golden handcuffs. And I was suffocating. On paper, I was living the life everyone said I should want. But every morning, as I looked in the mirror, the same thought crept in: *Is this it?* The question wasn't just about my job or my lifestyle, it was about everything. The endless meetings, the pursuit of the next promotion, the constant chase of more. More money, more status, more stuff. Yet somehow, it all added up to less. Less fulfillment. Less meaning. Less…life.

We all wrestle with these existential heavyweights: "Why am I here? What's my purpose? What am I really doing with my life?" Most of us bury these questions under emails and small talk, allowing them to sink into the quicksand of daily routines. But ignoring them doesn't make them disappear; it just buries them deeper. My wake-up call wasn't dramatic—no near-death experience or divine intervention— just the slow, creeping realization that I was climbing a ladder leaning against the wrong wall. The more I accomplished, the emptier I felt. I gradually realized that more work and more money led to less fulfillment. I was achieving, climbing, and collecting wins, yet something essential was missing. I had confused patterned motion with meaning. I was chasing more without ever asking whether it mattered. There was a growing tension inside me and the epiphany that I needed a way out.

The answer, it turned out, was hiding in plain sight. I was stuck in the unconscious trap of *doing* instead of *being*. Let that sink in for a moment: doing versus being. Sounds simple, right? Like most life-changing insights, it is, but it took me seventeen years to figure it out. I rebuilt slowly, piece by piece, like a human Lego set. Not with grand gestures but with small, steady acts: running one mile, writing one blog post, doing one more push-up when my arms were shaking, listening more, and talking less. It became a quiet practice. Over time, that practice became a life.

Putting the pieces together became a commitment to daily practices. A method that allowed me to shape and strengthen myself over time. Interestingly, I discovered that it worked surprisingly well. Goal setting turned into my guilty pleasure. I was in control, setting my own terms. It all had a reason, and it all started making sense. Then something unexpected happened: I started seeking out the things I said I'd never do. "I'll never stop eating meat." "I'll never run a marathon." "I'll never write a book." "I'll never give up alcohol." Each "never" became a dare—a silent challenge to push further. And the more impossible the goal seemed, the more alive I felt. A marathon a month for a year? Check. CEO? Done. Plant-based? Yep. I had turned "never" into done. And somewhere along the way, I stopped being surprised by what I could do. I was transforming, and I became a believer that I was capable of so much more than I'd imagined.

Think about the great explorers such as Lewis and Clark, Edmund Hillary, and Neil Armstrong. They heard "never" and thought, *watch me*. That same fire burns in all of us, even if we are not aware of it, even if it is dormant. It's not just dopamine or brain chemistry; it's the fundamental human drive to push beyond our limits, to become more than we are. Yet most of us live in what I call "primitive survival mode." That is, barely keeping our heads above water in an ocean of abundance. We're surprisingly good at doing nothing, avoiding challenges, and crafting elaborate excuses. We let the gravity of comfort pull us down, even as opportunities for growth float past like clouds. Is it oversimplifying to say that transformation starts with a shift in mindset? Maybe. But here's what I know: the choice to live intentionally—to truly live, not just exist—begins with a decision, your decision. In Maria Konnikova's *Mastermind: How to Think Like Sherlock Holmes*, she reminds us that "The most powerful mind is the quiet mind. It is the mind that is present, reflective, mindful of its thoughts and its state."[1] Well, that's what this life is all about.

THE POWER OF *YES*

Throughout this book, we'll explore what it truly means to live with intention. But at its core, intentional living often comes down to a deceptively simple idea: the direction of your life is shaped by the difference between *yes* and *no*. No is easy, safe, and keeps us anchored in the familiar. It stalls learning, keeps us safe, and we miss opportunities. *No* can protect us, but it can also trap us in comfort, fear, and habit. *Yes*, on the other hand, is where life begins to open. It is fulfillment, meaning, and purpose. *Yes* is motion. *Yes* is the door to growth, to learning, to possibility. It is where we thrive, but here's the part most people miss: *Yes* is only the beginning. *Yes* is the spark, but it's not the engine. When the excitement fades, when the road gets messy, *yes* alone isn't enough. To keep going, to go deeper, we need something more.

We need our *why*.

Our *why* is our north star—a deeply personal, internal compass that gives our life direction and meaning. It's more than a goal or ambition. It's the reason behind our choices, the quiet force that moves us when everything else feels stuck. It offers clarity in the chaos and purpose in the fog and reminds us that what we're building is something larger than ourselves. It's both a lens and a guide. A way to see the world and a way to navigate it. To live with a *why* is to align our daily actions, choices, and mindset with what truly matters to us. It doesn't mean we chase perfection. It means we choose to live in alignment with what we value the most. It means we move through the world with intention, even when things get hard. Especially when they get hard. That's how effort becomes fulfillment. That's how obstacles become fuel. That's how meaning shows up every day, in every way.

And in a world overflowing with curated images and filtered lives, it's more important than ever to remember: Our *why* isn't about what others see. It's not about applause or approval. It's not about followers or likes. It's about that quiet knowing inside and the answer to the questions: "What am I willing to suffer for? What makes me feel most alive? What would I still choose, even if no one else noticed?" It's where intention begins, and that's where we begin.

WHY OUR *WHY* MATTERS

Without a clear *why*, life becomes a series of reactions instead of intentional choices. We become wedded to routine, moving from task to task, trying to keep up with the demands of life without ever asking: "Why does this matter?" We might feel successful on paper with career wins, financial stability, and social recognition, but inside, there's a quiet emptiness. That's the danger of chasing achievement without purpose. A clear *why* transforms the grind into meaning. It makes the hard days bearable because we know what we are working toward. It turns setbacks into lessons because we know why we are showing up. When our *why* is strong enough, obstacles stop being reasons to quit; they become part of the path.

Research by psychologists like Dr. Michael Steger, who developed the Meaning in Life Questionnaire, shows that people who feel a strong sense of purpose tend to report higher life satisfaction, greater optimism, and lower depression.[2] Purpose gives us direction, and with direction comes motivation. When we pursue meaningful goals, our brain's reward system engages, helping reinforce those behaviors through feel-good chemicals like dopamine. It's not just philosophy; it's biology aligning with intention.

It's not coincidental that people with a strong *why* often report feeling energized and motivated, even in the face of significant challenges. Purpose isn't just an abstract concept; it's a physiological and psychological driver that propels us toward growth and fulfillment.

THE LINK BETWEEN *YES* AND *WHY*

Yes is the moment of courage. It's the leap of faith when you don't know how things will turn out. But your *why* is the foundation beneath that leap. It's the thing that allows you to push forward even after you fall. *Yes* without *why* is shallow. You can say *yes* to a big goal or a new opportunity, but if your *why* isn't strong enough, you'll falter when the excitement fades. Without a clear *why*, every obstacle feels like a reason to stop. But when your *why* is clear, challenges become fuel. Think about a marathon. Saying *yes* is showing up at the starting line.

Your *why* is what gets you through mile twenty when your legs are screaming and your mind is begging you to stop. *Yes* gets you moving. *Why* keeps you running. Your *why* makes *yes* sustainable. *Yes* is the spark. *Why* is the engine.

THE COURAGE TO DEFINE YOUR *WHY*

Defining our *why* takes courage because it requires us to be brutally honest with ourselves. It's not about what other people expect of us. It's not about what looks good on paper. It's about what feels authentic in our bones. Most of us spend too much time chasing someone else's version of success. We climb ladders we don't actually care about. We pursue goals that aren't ours because they seem impressive or important. And we wonder why we feel unfulfilled even when we "succeed."

Many years ago, it struck me that I am not here to live the life that others are choosing for me. I am here to live the life of my choosing. It hit me like a thunderbolt on an ordinary Wednesday afternoon. A group of colleagues was heading to the usual after-work watering hole. "Come with us," they insisted, packing up their backpacks. "This is where the real networking happens." I paused, then made a counteroffer that surprised even me: "How about we go for a run instead? Five miles along the canal. We can network, talk business, solve the world's problems—just without the bar tab." They laughed like I'd suggested we fly to Mars. "No way," they said, shaking their heads. "You're crazy." So, they went "left" to the bar and I went "right," lacing up my running shoes. In that moment, that simple choice between their path and mine, I found the first thread of what would become my authentic life. It wasn't only about running versus drinking. It

was about choosing my own direction instead of following the worn
path of habit and others' expectations.

> Many years ago, it struck me that I am not here
> to live the life that others are choosing for
> me. I am here to live the life of my choosing.

Living intentionally, I've learned, requires a kind of stripped-down
honesty that most of us spend our lives avoiding. It demands that
we stand naked before the mirror of our own life and ask the question that makes us squirm: "What do I really want?" Not what my
LinkedIn profile says I should want. Not what my parents dreamed
for me. Not what society rewards with corner offices and big houses.
But what would make my soul feel like it has finally come home?
That's where our *why* lives. It's in that raw, quiet space beneath the
noise of "shoulds" and "supposed tos." It's in the courage to choose
our own direction, even when everyone else is heading to the bar.

But how do we uncover our *why*? Sometimes it emerges from a
loss that reshaped us, a moment of failure that forced us to confront
what really matters. Other times it's born from joy, a breakthrough, a
moment when we feel fully alive. It's not about perfection; it's about
our true selves. It might be rooted in family, providing for loved ones,
or building a foundation for the next generation. For others, it's about
helping others, personal growth, creativity, or making a difference in
the world. Also, our *why* doesn't have to be grand or world-changing;
it simply must resonate deeply within us. We can start with questions that matter to us. What drives us? What makes us feel alive?
What are we willing to fight for, to sacrifice for? And perhaps most

importantly, what kind of legacy do we want to leave behind? (By the way, it is never too early to start thinking about legacy.) The good news is that our *why* isn't a one-time exercise; it's a living, evolving process. As life shifts, so might our purpose—and that's okay. The goal isn't meant to be rigid but to provide clarity, even if that clarity evolves. It's tempting to think that finding our *why* is about creating a life plan or setting big, audacious goals. But it's deeper than that. Our *why* isn't defined by achievement; it's defined by alignment. Are we living in a way that reflects our core values? Are we creating a life that feels true to who we are?

This is where it starts: just you, a blank page, and complete honesty. Just write what comes to mind, your *why*. Not the polished version you'd share on social media, but the raw reality that surfaces when you let your guard down. The first time I did this, my hand trembled slightly. It felt like opening a door I wasn't sure I was ready to walk through. But here's what I discovered: your *why* isn't carved in stone. It's more like a garden, that is, something you tend to, something that grows and evolves. I return to mine regularly, not to judge it, but to nurture it. Sometimes, I add something new; other times, I prune away what no longer serves. Each time I write it down, each time I speak it aloud, I'm recommitting to the path I've chosen.

Let me be clear about something: defining your *why* isn't about crafting the perfect mission statement. It's not about impressing anyone or winning awards for eloquence. It's about creating a north star that guides you home when you're lost in the noise of daily life. Think of it as laying down breadcrumbs for your future self, markers that remind you of what matters when the world tries to distract you with shiny objects and false urgencies. When you align your life with your *why*, something magical happens. The smallest actions take on new meaning. That early morning workout isn't just about burning calories; it's about building the strength to serve others better. That extra hour spent mastering a skill isn't just about professional development; it's about expanding your capacity to make a difference in ways that deeply align with your values.

Defining your *why* isn't about crafting the perfect mission statement. It's not about impressing anyone or winning awards for eloquence. It's about creating a north star that guides you home when you're lost in the noise of daily life.

After years of refinement, my own *why* has distilled into something that both grounds and propels me: I build myself to build others. Every capability I develop becomes a ladder someone else can climb. Every insight I gain becomes a light I can share. My pursuit of self-discovery has not been just for me; it's about creating a blueprint others can follow, adapt, and improve upon. It's about service and potential and about supporting others as they move from ordinary to extraordinary. This is the power of a well-defined *why*: it transforms everything it touches. Our decisions become clearer. Our priorities sharpen. Our days are filled with purpose instead of just tasks. And slowly but surely, we move from simply existing to truly living: intentionally, consciously, purposefully, and authentically.

It's interesting to reflect on how my *why* became so clear, how I arrived at this point of wanting to serve others and help them achieve their potential. On one level, it's obvious: I'm paying it forward for all the help and support I received throughout my career. It feels like just yesterday when Mark, a partner at the accounting company Ernst &

Young, included me in discussions typically reserved for more senior people. I felt supported and seen, and that experience showed me the power of helping unlock the potential in each of us. So, it feels necessary, almost like a contract with the universe, a way of setting myself up to give back. But more than anything, my service mindset was shaped by my parents. My dad was a social worker in New York City schools for over thirty years, working with troubled youth. My mom worked for Child Protective Services and the Office for the Aging, always serving people in need. I learned early on that this is what we do: we take care of each other. I've often joked with my dad that I'm a social worker too; the only difference is that the people I worked with wore ties and suits and walked around thinking they were important. But the principle is the same. I deeply appreciate the role models my parents were, and I wish everyone had the benefit of such a strong foundation. It would be almost impossible for me not to build on the lessons I learned at home. We're here to take care of each other. That's what I live for, even when it gets hard.

My *why* isn't just words on paper—it's a battle cry. I am here to help others rise, to guide them as they step into their full power and glimpse the vast landscape of their potential. But here's the thing about battle cries: they mean nothing if you haven't been in the trenches yourself. I knew that if I was going to serve others, that is, *really* serve them, not just dispense coffee-mug wisdom, then I needed to prove my *why* in the crucible of experience. I needed to find my impossible. The search for my impossible was like trying to catch smoke. Climb Everest? An incredible challenge, but it felt like borrowing someone else's dream. Run across America? Tempting, but life doesn't pause for months while you chase horizons. I wanted something raw, something mostly unsupported, a test of pure resilience that would fit into the constraints of a regular life. Something that would force me to confront that three a.m. moment when every fiber of my being screams *quit*.

Then it hit me, during yet another late-night flight, staring out at the darkness enveloping the horizon. The idea came in a whisper that grew to a roar. I'm a runner. I love to travel and have logged more air miles than I can count. What if I combined these two pieces of my life into something that seemed absurd, even to me? Run six marathons. On six continents. In six consecutive days. I pulled a pad and pen from my backpack and wrote it down. My hand trembled. The words stared back at me, both beautiful and terrifying. It would mean 26.2 miles, six times over, with international flights squeezed between each run. The logistics alone were daunting. The physical toll would be brutal. The mental game? Uncharted territory. It was perfect. Perfect because it scared me. Perfect because it lived in that sweet spot between impossible and barely possible, the exact space where transformation happens. Perfect because when I mentioned it to others, they looked at me like I'd lost my mind. The nine months that followed weren't just about training. They were about becoming and intentionally working towards a goal. Every pre-dawn run, every strength session, and every calorie consumed was building more than just physical capacity. I was constructing a living example of human potential, testing the limits of what's possible when you refuse to accept conventional boundaries.

This wasn't just another endurance challenge. This was my crucible, the forge where I would either prove my *why* or watch it crumble. Because if you are going to serve others through their darkness, it is difficult to do so if you've never found your way through your own. You can't help others push their limits if you're not willing to explore yours. This insane, audacious goal became my way of earning the right to say, "I can help you walk the path because I've walked it. I know the dragons because I've faced them. And I'm here to go with you through your own impossible."

As I reflected on the challenge, I couldn't shake off the feeling of the popular saying, "your new life will cost you your old one." Chasing your *why* means leaving comfort behind. It requires letting go of the familiar and stepping into the unknown. The life I wanted, one defined by service and impact, would cost me the life I once knew. But it was a price I was willing to pay. And that's the thing about pursuing your *why*: it's not just about knowing it; it's about having the courage to chase it, even when it demands sacrifice. That's why the six-marathon challenge wasn't merely a physical test; it represented a symbolic shift. It was me letting go of the old life, the one built solely on career achievement and financial success, and stepping into a new identity defined by service and contribution. The real test wasn't the miles; it was the willingness to let go of comfort and ego to lean into a better version of myself.

I remember hearing ultra-endurance athlete and podcaster Rich Roll reflect on the transformative power of discomfort. He emphasized that you can't hack discipline or shortcut hard work, but what you *can* do is learn to fall in love with the process of becoming.[3] That idea stuck with me. The goal isn't to avoid the struggle; it's to embrace it as the very thing that shapes us. That's exactly what those six marathons taught me. There's no shortcut to discovering your *why*. It's not about chasing the finish line; it's about learning to love the journey. It's about showing up when it's hard, trusting the process when the outcome isn't clear, and embracing the discomfort along the way. Because that's the heart of living intentionally: it's not about the destination; it's about becoming the kind of person who's brave enough to take the first step, and every step after that. I completed the challenge, and the feeling of illumination was real. My intentions emerged in a very real way, meaning and purpose were no longer just words. They had become life itself, woven into who I was becoming. It became a springboard for leaning into my *why* and realizing that the power within is immense; I just needed to tap into it.

With a strong foundation from my own lived experience, I began to see how others live in alignment with their *why*: clearly, courageously, and often quietly. Malala Yousafzai's purpose, to fight for girls' education, was born from her own experience and the injustice she witnessed. Despite threats, violence, and nearly losing her life, she never wavered.[4] Her story reminds us that when we're rooted in purpose, even a single voice can shake the world.

One of my personal heroes, Ernest Shackleton, showed us another form of *why*, one forged in leadership and loyalty. When his ship, *Endurance*, was crushed by Antarctic ice, he made one decision and never let go: every member of his crew would survive. For nearly two years, he carried that purpose across frozen oceans and impossible odds. He didn't just lead an expedition; he held lives in his hands and never looked away.[5]

LOVE AS A WAY OF LIVING

Not all *whys* roar from podiums or blaze across headlines. Some live in quiet rooms, in unseen acts of love and steadiness. Anthea, my wife, is one of the most intentional people I know, not because she declares it, but because she lives it every single day. Her purpose was never about chasing status or acclaim; it was about presence—showing up fully, fiercely, and with an open heart. She anchored our family with a strength so consistent that it was easy to overlook, but it was always there in the ways she held space for our daughters' dreams, the meals made with care, the late-night talks, and the unwavering belief she poured into the family she loved. There were no viral quotes, no magazine features—just a life lived with profound intention. A *why* rooted in love, resilience, and a kind of presence that doesn't need to be loud to be powerful. Our girls are who they are today, not just because of *what* Anthea did, but because of *how* she did it: with grace, with conviction, and with a level of devotion that shapes generations.

It reminds me that living intentionally isn't always about massive reinventions or grand gestures. Sometimes, it's about showing up every day with love at the center.

That, too, is a legacy. That, too, is a *why* worth honoring. It just has to be *real*. A purpose grounded in what matters, whether it's raising a family, protecting your team, speaking out, or staying true to yourself, has the power to shape a life. And that's more than enough.

LIVING MY *WHY*

Over the course of ninety marathons and ultras, I built more than endurance; I built perspective. Every race, every mile, every early morning taught me something about resilience, self-doubt, and the quiet courage required to keep going. What began as a personal pursuit slowly evolved into something greater. I wasn't just collecting medals; I was preparing to serve. All those experiences became the foundation for something far more meaningful: helping others discover what they were capable of. My *why*, rooted in service, support, and belief in human potential, came alive not at the end of my own races but in the moments I stood beside someone running their first.

Now, when someone shares a dream of running their first marathon or stepping into the unknown of an ultra, I feel that familiar spark. I see in their eyes the same blend of hope and hesitation I once knew so well. Training plans become more than just prescriptions for mileage; they become a map for transformation. Early morning texts of encouragement, late-night check-ins, and adjusting the plan when life throws a curveball—these aren't tasks; they're sacred steps in someone else's becoming. Sometimes, I'm there on race day, pacing them through the hardest miles. I've learned when to offer words and when presence is enough. And when they cross that finish line—whether it's their first marathon or a hundred grueling miles—something extraordinary happens. In their victory, my *why* comes alive. Their joy, their disbelief, their "I can't believe I did it"— those moments hold more meaning than any medal I've ever earned.

My purpose was never just about running. It was about standing beside someone as they meet the edge of who they thought they were, and step beyond it. It was about being the voice that whispers "keep going" when every part of them wants to stop. It was about helping rewrite the story they tell themselves about what's possible. My *why* was never meant to live in theory. It was meant to be lived in the quiet moments of support, in the encouragement shared mile after mile, and in the transformation I witness when someone realizes they're capable of more. That's the gift of living with purpose: it turns everyday actions into something sacred. And that's what I want for you. Not just to define your *why*, but to bring it to life. To embody it. To share it. To let it guide how you move through the world, and how you help others do the same.

WHAT'S YOUR *WHY*?

To discover it, you need to give yourself the time and space to reflect. Ask yourself the hard questions, sit with the discomfort, and be willing to repeat this process again and again. Writing it down isn't just helpful; it's essential. There's something about putting your *why* into words that makes it real. Sometimes it takes a long walk or quiet time to get the process going. If it feels hard, that's okay. Growth isn't supposed to be easy. To help you get started, I've included some prompts below, but remember, your *why* isn't something you can force. It's something you uncover. Once you've written it down, try reading it out loud. There's power in hearing your own voice speak your *why*. It's one thing to think about your *why*; it's another to hear it. When you speak it out loud, you'll know if it feels aligned or if something's off. That's part of the process. You might need to refine it or adjust it over time, and that's okay, too. There's no right or wrong when it comes to your *why*. It just needs to be *yours*. The more honest you are with yourself, the more powerful your *why* will be.

The good news is that you'll go from novice to expert in this process, but no matter how clear your *why* becomes, you'll need to keep working on and refining it. Your *why* isn't static; it evolves as you grow. Life will test it. Circumstances will challenge it. But once you've defined it, living it becomes the work of a lifetime, and that's where the magic of intentional living begins.

PUTTING IT INTO PRACTICE

Defining your *why* is the starting point of intentional living. It's your opportunity to lean into what life can become. With clarity of purpose, you'll find the strength and inspiration to build a life that reflects your values, passions, and potential. To define your *why*, begin with reflection and structured exercises. Lean in. Take the first step and have fun doing it. Here's a step-by-step process to help you uncover it:

1. Ask Big Questions

Start with these foundational questions:

- **What impact do I want to have?**—What change do I want to create in the world or the lives of others?

- **What do I want to experience?**—What moments, feelings, or experiences make me feel most alive?

- **Who do I want to become?**—What qualities do I want to embody, regardless of success or failure?

Tip: If you feel most alive when mentoring others, your *why* might center on empowering people to reach their potential.

2. Identify Patterns

Look for recurring themes in your answers. Are they tied to helping others, creating, achieving, or exploring?

- If creativity and problem-solving are what energize you, your *why* might focus on using innovation to make a difference.

- If connection and empathy come through, your *why* might be about building meaningful relationships or supporting others through challenges.

Tip: If you're drawn to creative problem-solving, your *why* could be: *To inspire new ways of thinking through creativity and innovation.*

3. Distill It

Write a one-sentence statement that captures your *why*. Keep it simple and clear.

- If you're deeply connected to nature and sustainability, your *why* might be: *To inspire a deeper respect for the natural world and advocate for sustainable living.*

- If helping others motivates you, it could be: *To empower others to unlock their potential and live intentionally.*

Tip: If it feels too complicated, you're overthinking it. Your *why* should feel like a natural reflection of who you are.

4. Test It

Use your *why* as a lens for decision-making over the next week.

- Does it guide you?

- Does it feel aligned with your choices?

- Does it give you clarity when faced with uncertainty?

Tip: If your *why* is to foster meaningful relationships, notice how it influences your conversations and interactions. If it doesn't feel right, refine it.

5. Revisit It Regularly

Your *why* isn't fixed; it evolves as you grow. Life changes, priorities shift, and new experiences shape your perspective.

- Schedule time every few months to reflect and refine your *why*.

- If your circumstances shift, like starting a family or taking on a new career, your *why* may need to adjust.

Tip: If you once defined your *why* around career success but find more meaning in raising a family, your *why* might shift toward supporting and nurturing others.

POTENTIAL PITFALLS AND MISSTEPS

Defining your *why* isn't always straightforward. Here are some common traps to avoid:

- **Seeking Perfection**

  » Your *why* doesn't have to be flawless. It's okay if it evolves over time. Don't let the pursuit of perfection prevent you from starting.

- **Confusing Your *Why* with Your Goals**

  » Your *why* is about purpose, not achievement. Goals are milestones; your *why* is the driving force behind them.

- **Comparing Yourself to Others**

  » Your *why* is yours alone. Don't measure it against someone else's path.

- **Overthinking It**

  » Sometimes the simplest answers are the most profound. Trust your instincts and focus on what truly resonates with you. You don't need permission from anyone to justify your *why*.

CHAPTER 2

BUILDING OUR PILLARS

The Power of Consistency

There's a quiet force in our lives, often overlooked in a world obsessed with hacks and highlight reels. It's not flashy. It doesn't trend. But it builds character, strengthens resolve, and turns intention into reality. That force is consistency. Most of what's meaningful in life isn't built in bursts of inspiration; it's built in moments of discipline. The choice to show up repeatedly, especially when we don't feel like it, is where our real foundation is laid. Consistency isn't about perfection; it's about process. It's about honoring the path when no one's watching, when it would be easier to quit, and when progress feels invisible. Whether nurturing a relationship, mastering a skill, or rebuilding our health, results don't come from what we do once; they come from what we do repeatedly. Just as water sculpts stone, our smallest daily actions shape who we become. Extraordinary outcomes aren't born from sudden bursts of effort; they emerge from the quiet rhythm of repetition. That's where transformation lives.

LIVING YOUR *WHY*, DAY BY DAY

I used to think having a clear *why* was enough. Spoiler alert: it's not. Purpose without action is like having a map but never taking the trip. For years, I was that person with big dreams and endless excuses. You probably know the dance: start strong on Monday, fade by Wednesday, promise yourself next week will be different. Work deadlines, family obligations, and going out with friends all seemed more urgent than my goals. I became an expert at justifying why today wasn't the right day to start living intentionally. Sound familiar?

What I didn't understand then was that having a *why* isn't the finish line; it's the starting point. To *live* our *why*, we need structure. We need architecture. We need pillars: strong, dependable supports that can withstand the storms of daily life and anchor us when we begin to drift. Without these, even the most inspiring purpose gets buried beneath the noise of modern living.

Whether by grace, luck, or desperation, my breakthrough came from an unexpected place: a simple leadership moment. One day, in either a burst of courage or a lapse in sanity, I posted a message in my company newsletter. "I'm going to work out three days a week," I wrote, putting myself on record in front of the whole company, Mainspring. And just to raise the stakes, I added, "I'll track it in a spreadsheet so anyone can see it." The minute that email went out, I felt the weight of what I'd done. I hadn't worked out consistently even once a week, and now I'd publicly committed to three. But that public declaration did something important; it turned a vague desire into a lived commitment.

I'm not saying those first few weeks were easy, far from it. I kept wondering how I was going to keep this up with everything else on my plate. But that simple spreadsheet became my first real accountability partner. Those empty cells stared at me, daring me to follow through. And the thought of facing my colleagues without doing what I said I would do? That was more motivating than any quote on discipline could ever be. It wasn't fancy, just a basic Excel file with dates and checkboxes, but it worked. I had no idea then that I would keep it up for the next twenty-five years. To this day, I still fill out that spreadsheet every single morning, watching those small marks of consistency add up to profound change.

Here's what I've learned: we are wired for accountability but not always for self-discipline. From our earliest days, we follow structures built by others—parents with bedtime rules, teachers with homework deadlines, bosses with deliverables. So, when it comes time to hold ourselves accountable, we often struggle.

The good news? Accountability doesn't have to mean hiring a coach or joining a program. It can be as simple as a journal, a fitness tracker, or a text thread with a friend. The tool doesn't matter. What matters is that it makes your commitments *real* and your progress *visible.* My spreadsheet wasn't just about working out anymore—it was my first intentional pillar. It proved to me that I could keep the promises I made to myself. It showed me how structure could turn my *why* from a hopeful idea into a sustainable way of living.

GRIT, GRACE, AND GROUNDEDNESS OR G³: THE PILLARS OF LIVING INTENTIONALLY

Defining our *why* gives us direction. Building habits and creating accountability ensure that we stay aligned with it. But to truly sustain intentional living over the long haul, we need something deeper, something that strengthens and empowers us from within. I worked in the city of skyscrapers, New York City, for many years, and I admired the massiveness of iconic buildings like the Empire State and the Woolworth Building. As I learned, before they could reach for the sky, their builders had to dig deep, sometimes hundreds of feet down to find the bedrock, so they could set a foundation strong enough to allow them to be taller than any other buildings and withstand anything nature might throw at them. Living intentionally demands the same kind of engineering. We need an inner architecture robust enough to support our highest aspirations and weather life's hurricanes.

This is where G^3 comes in: Grit, Grace, and Groundedness. These aren't just inspirational words for my coffee mug. It is a life architecture that has evolved from my lived and earned experiences. They characterize my version of the steel beams that we need to live a life built on purpose. They are the "rebar" that reinforces every decision, every action, every moment when it would be easier to quit than continue. Later, we'll explore the other essential pillars of intentional living (exercise, nutrition, sleep, mindset, and community). But first, we need to understand how G^3 weaves together like strands of a rope, each strengthening the others, creating a foundation that can hold the weight of our biggest dreams and our heaviest burdens. The beauty of G^3 is that it's already within you. You don't need to order it, download it, or buy it. You just need to uncover it and use it to strengthen your pillars. And that construction project starts now.

GRIT: THE BACKBONE OF PERSEVERANCE

Grit is the unyielding spirit that drives us to keep going, even when the odds are stacked against us. Picture this: It's 5 a.m. It's raining. Your bed is warm, and your running shoes are cold; the alarm rings, and the snooze button is one push away. This is where grit lives, in that space between comfort and growth, between what's easy and what's necessary. Grit isn't about being tough all the time. It's not about grinding yourself to dust or pushing through injury and exhaustion. No, grit is simpler and more profound than that. It's about showing up when every fiber of your being is voting for comfort. It's about doing the small, unsexy work that nobody sees but everybody feels.

While talent and intelligence may open doors, it is grit, the ability to persevere over the long haul, that ensures we walk through them. Angela Duckworth's research revealed something that every successful person knows in their bones: the students who succeed aren't always the smartest. They're the ones who keep showing up, the ones who say, "Yes, I can" instead of "No, I can't." Their secret wasn't talent; it was perseverance over time.[1]

I've lived this for over twenty-five years, one spreadsheet cell at a time. That accountability system I mentioned? Still going strong. Not because I'm special, but because I made showing up non-negotiable. This is what I mean by a "lived and earned" experience. Each check mark, each completed workout, each small victory, is another brick in the foundation of who I'm becoming. And through it all, across more than five million miles of travel, the spreadsheet traveled with me. It became part logbook, part motivator. Writing down that I went for a run in Malaysia or Barcelona added some joy to the process. It kept my goals front and center and made me think ahead— *What will I do when the plane lands in a new city?* I began to think of grit as a muscle. And like any muscle, it grows stronger with use. The key wasn't heroic moments, though there were a few, like landing at 10:30 p.m. in Tokyo and deciding to run around the Imperial Palace at midnight to check the box. The real magic was in the quiet decision I made every day, a thousand times over, to do what needed to be done.

GRACE: YOUR SECRET STRENGTH

Grace isn't what most people think it is. It's not about being delicate or diplomatic. It's not about perfect posture or polite conversation. Grace is a profound strength, the medicine we all need to take, so we can be gentle with ourselves when the world expects perfection. It took me a long time to lean into the essence and power of grace. My long-time mentor, John, told me many times, "You better learn how to celebrate on the way to success because you are never going to get there." Those words play back in my head again and again. I learned that I need to approach my evolution with grace so that I could celebrate the small victories (and the big ones, too), find wisdom in my stumbles, and see setbacks (too many to list) not as dead ends but as detours that might lead somewhere even better. While grit pushes us forward, grace gives us permission to pause, reflect, and recalibrate. It's the voice that says, "This too is part of the path," when life doesn't give us exactly what we want. Grace transforms regret from poison to medicine. Instead of letting past mistakes haunt us like angry ghosts, grace helps us see them as chapters in our story, not failures to be buried, but experiences that shaped who we're becoming. I now tell myself that since I was there for the decision, I can have no regret about what I did, just responsibility and grace, and with this in mind, I feel the burden of regret fade away.

Consider a parent balancing the demands of a career and raising children. There will inevitably be moments of frustration, mistakes, and feelings of inadequacy. Grace is the tool that allows them to step back and say, "I'm doing my best, and that's enough." Dr. Brené Brown, a leading researcher on vulnerability and shame, emphasizes that perfectionism is not the same as striving for excellence. Instead, it's a shield that keeps us from true connection and growth. By embracing imperfection and focusing on love and effort rather than flawless execution, parents not only cultivate resilience in themselves but also model self-compassion for their children. In doing so, they teach the next generation that mistakes are not failures but opportunities to learn, adapt, and grow. [2]

I witnessed this transformation in my own home through what we came to know as "the pink robe strategy." My wife, Anthea, had this simple but brilliant signal with our daughters, Julianne and Kimberly: when she wore her pink robe, it meant she was tired and would lead with love instead of perfection. This wasn't just about comfortable clothing; it became a powerful shorthand for "I'm human, you're human, let's be kind to each other." Simple? Yes. Revolutionary? Absolutely. That pink robe created a space where grace could flourish, allowing three humans to give each other permission to be beautifully imperfect.

Roger Federer captured the theme of grace beautifully in his 2024 Dartmouth commencement speech. Tennis, he explained, is a game where errors far outnumber perfect shots. Even the greatest players in the world spend most of their time missing. Success isn't about avoiding mistakes; it's about making peace with them and learning to see them as teachers. [3] Federer's career exemplifies this: after his most crushing defeats, he's shown grace that transforms loss into legacy. Whether facing heartbreaking defeats at Wimbledon or celebrating his greatest victories, his composure reminds us that true greatness isn't just about skill, it's about how we carry ourselves through both triumph and tribulation.

This is the paradox of grace, that it's both gentle and powerful. It allows us to hold two truths at once: we are works in progress, and we are enough exactly as we are. When we embrace this paradox, we find a different kind of strength, not the hard-edged force of pure grit, but the supple power of a river that knows how to flow around obstacles instead of always trying to break through them.

GROUNDEDNESS: THE ANCHOR OF PURPOSE

Think of groundedness as a GPS of sorts, not the kind that tells you where to go, but the kind that reminds you who you are. While grit drives us forward and grace helps us learn from our stumbles, groundedness keeps us anchored to what matters most. Groundedness is about integrity, that is, making sure that the way we live matches the values we hold. It's the ability to ask ourselves, "Does this action reflect who I want to be and what I stand for?"

My own grounding ritual might sound strange at first. Every morning, I tell myself, "Today is a vacation day." Not because I'm planning to lounge by a pool, but because this simple phrase changes everything. It transforms my mindset from a list of obligations to a series of choices. Meetings become opportunities. Challenges become adventures. Going for a run is a treat. Even mundane tasks take on new meaning when viewed through this lens of conscious choice and shift in perspective rather than hard labor.

Fred Rogers understood this kind of groundedness better than most. In the world of television that increasingly favored flash over substance, Rogers chose to move at the speed of childhood. He began each day by praying for others by name, maintained his gentle demeanor despite industry pressure to be more "entertaining," and never wavered from his mission to nurture children's emotional well-being. While others chased ratings, Rogers remained anchored to his purpose: helping children feel seen, heard, and valued.[4]

Perhaps no recent example illustrates the power of groundedness more clearly than Simone Biles at the 2020 Tokyo Olympics. There she stood on the world's biggest stage, carrying the weight of a nation's expectations. The old script would have demanded she push through at any cost. Instead, Biles chose to listen to her inner compass. Her decision to step back wasn't about giving up; it was about standing firm when the whole world was pushing her to do otherwise. In that moment, Biles demonstrated what groundedness truly means. It's not about being unshakeable. It's about knowing what to hold onto when everything around you is shaking. It's about having the courage to disappoint others rather than betray yourself.[5]

Groundedness is about alignment. It's the internal compass that keeps us steady when life pulls us in every direction. It's the difference between being driven by external expectations and being guided by internal purpose. The sales guy in me knows this all too well. I've been in those moments: quarter-end closing, deal almost done, just a day late. The temptation to change the date, to make the numbers look good, is always there. But groundedness makes the choice clear. We report what happened, not what we wish had happened. We lead with integrity. Because in the long run, we're not here to live up to someone else's definition of success, we're here to stay true to our own.

THE POWER OF THE TRIFECTA

If consistency is the architecture of intentional living, then G^3—grit, grace, and groundedness—are the pillars that hold it up. These aren't abstract values; they're living forces that shape how we show up every day. They're what help us stay aligned when things get hard, uncertain, or messy. After years of practicing intentional habits, I began to see that what sustained me wasn't just structure, it was who I was becoming because of how I responded in the moment. That's what G³ is all about: building the capacity to keep going, stay open, and remain clear-headed in the face of challenge. We've laid the foundation. Now, let's bring these pillars to life and explore how grit, grace, and groundedness manifest in the moments that shape us.

Grit Fuels Perseverance: It enables us to tackle obstacles head-on, building resilience and fortitude.

- As an entrepreneur launching a startup, I found out that rejection is an inevitable part of the process. Early in my entrepreneurial career, I traveled to the legendary Sand Hill Road in Silicon Valley to raise capital, convinced that investors would recognize the brilliance of my company, Exit41, and be excited to invest in our big vision. Instead, I left with little more than a chorus of "Good luck" and "Not right now." Returning to our office in Andover, MA, I had a choice—dwell on the rejection or use it as fuel. I chose the latter, refining my pitch, learning from every "no," and pressing forward. It took no less than thirty more meetings before I secured funding. My team joked that my "grit score" improved with every rejection, but persistence was the reason we ultimately succeeded.

Grace Fosters Growth: It teaches us to learn from setbacks and approach life with humility and compassion.

- My good friend Ryan, a high school history teacher, has shared his strategy for managing cell phone use in the classroom. Rather than resorting to frustration or punishment, he approaches it with grace by offering polite but firm reminders that students are there to learn. He recognizes that cell phones are deeply embedded in teenage life, but rather than fighting this reality, he meets it with understanding. His approach not only reduces tension in the classroom but also encourages students to engage with their education more intentionally. Grace allows him to lead by setting proper expectations and having patience that fosters a more constructive learning environment for everyone.

Groundedness Provides Clarity: It anchors us to our purpose, ensuring that our efforts are meaningful and aligned.

- Building software is always a challenge. There are more customer requests than we can deliver, and an ever-present expectation that everything happens fast. I was at Exit41, the first time I was CEO of a software company, and we were racing to release a new version of our platform that we had not tested thoroughly enough. What we shipped was buggy, and our customers were understandably unhappy. But instead of reacting with panic, I returned to the core approach that's served me well: assess the situation, listen carefully to the customer, develop a plan, communicate clearly about how we'll fix the problem, do the work, and deploy with care. That steady rhythm kept both our team and our customers from spiraling. The problems didn't disappear overnight, but that grounded process gave us the clarity and energy to face them head-on and fix them. We got it done. And staying grounded made all the difference.

Living intentionally isn't about the words; it's about how we live them. G^3 enables a different kind of resilience, one that's not just about enduring hardship but about thriving in the face of it. It's building resilience guided by purpose and made sustainable because we've defined our pillars and integrated them into our daily lives.

WHY DAILY PRACTICE MATTERS

Living intentionally begins with translating the values of grit, grace, and groundedness into daily practices. That is, small actions that, over time, write the story of who we are becoming. Our practices stabilize us, providing structure and focus in a chaotic world. Daily practices are the mortar that holds our internal structure together. More than that, they serve as a constant reminder of what matters most. When we commit to small, meaningful actions every day, we create momentum. These practices are the bridge between our aspirations and our reality.

Writing a book isn't just about one brilliant idea or a burst of inspiration; it's about showing up every day. It's about putting down one word, one sentence, one paragraph at a time. There are days when it flows and days when it doesn't, but the act of returning to the page is what defines a writer. Our purpose works the same way. Daily practices are like sentences: individually small, yet together, they create something meaningful. Over time, they form a narrative, the narrative of who we are becoming. I may not have known the ending when I began, but I've created something enduring by writing a little each day.

What if we were to think about our daily habits as foundational as eating, sleeping, and brushing our teeth? What if we made a set of good-for-us daily practices so ingrained that we don't even question them? My experience tells me that life changes in a profound and measurable way when we do. I've lived it. I've deliberately added two daily habits: exercise and writing. And when I look back across the past twenty-five years, the cumulative impact of these small, consistent actions is undeniable. I can confidently state that I am a productive writer, having written over five thousand pages, and a good runner, with over 55,000 miles run. That's staggering to think about. Sometimes I wonder, what if I had spent the past twenty-five years playing the piano? How good would I have become?

The power of a daily practice isn't just about skill; it's about identity. A daily habit doesn't just shape what we do; it shapes who we become. It crafts our capabilities in ways we can't fully appreciate until we step back and see what we've built. Here's the point: choose something and stick with it. A daily habit is a vote for the person you want to become. It's a quiet yet powerful declaration. *This matters to me. This is who I am becoming.*

James Clear, in *Atomic Habits*, emphasizes the 1 Percent Rule: how tiny, consistent improvements compound over time to produce extraordinary results.[6] I've lived by this approach for countless years. The good news is that the same principle applies to any habit: whether it's yoga every morning, a five-minute gratitude practice, or making hundreds of sales calls, consistency drives transformation. What we do daily ultimately defines who we become. But just as powerful is what we choose *not* to do. I've been alcohol-free for over twenty years, and the benefits—better sleep, more energy, sharper performance—have compounded just like my running and writing. Our daily practices are not only about progress; they're about identity.

If you do six Ironman races (like I have), you *are* an Ironman. Run sixty ultramarathons, and you *are* an ultramarathoner (me too). Make the President's Club in sales, and you *are* a rainmaker. When we show up every day for something, we reinforce a fundamental principle: *this is who I am.* Our daily practice becomes an expression of our values, shaping how we see ourselves and how others see us. A writer isn't someone who publishes a book; it's someone who writes every day. A runner isn't defined by a marathon; it's the person who laces up their shoes even when no race is in sight. I have experienced this firsthand. Every time I see someone I know—whether at work, among friends, or even a casual acquaintance—they ask me the same question: "Did you run today?"

That's how deep the connection is between habit and identity. My commitment to daily running hasn't just shaped my health and mindset, it's become part of how people see me. It's a reminder that when we commit to daily practices, we anchor ourselves to our greater purpose. No matter how unpredictable life becomes, these small, consistent actions remind us of who we are and what we stand for.

HOW DAILY PRACTICES BUILD RESILIENCE

Life is unpredictable, and tough times are inevitable. Resilience isn't about avoiding hardship; it's about having the strength to face it head-on. That strength comes from the foundation we build through consistent daily practices. During a particularly challenging year with one of my startups, I committed to doing 150,000 push-ups. Maybe not the smartest idea, but there I was. It meant about 410 push-ups a day, every day. Each set was a reminder of the commitment I made to myself, and that getting to the goal would require daily, consistent effort. The push-ups became the steady thread I could hold onto when everything else felt chaotic. No matter what happened each day, whether I felt strong or exhausted, I showed up.

Then came the moment of reckoning.

I had flown from Boston to Los Angeles. The flight was delayed, the Uber got lost, and I didn't reach my hotel until two a.m. With a 5:30 a.m. wake-up looming for my daily run, I started to get ready for bed when it hit me: I hadn't done my push-ups. I froze. My mind raced: *Maybe I don't need to do them? I did them yesterday. I'll double up tomorrow. No one will know.*

But then it hit me—*I made a promise. Not to anyone else. To myself.* And that had to mean something. It didn't matter how tired I was or how late it had gotten. So, I got down on the hotel floor and knocked out all of them. Then I went to bed, got up to run, and moved on with my day.

But something had changed.

I had crossed a line—the line we all face when we meet ourselves at the edge of a commitment. That's where resilience is built, not in grand, visible moments of triumph, but in the quiet decisions we make when no one's watching. That's the hidden gift of daily habits. They don't just track our progress; they create a baseline of strength that carries us through life's challenging moments. When the path gets tough, you lean on the person you've already become through those small, faithful actions. That's why consistency matters. It's not just shaping what you do—it's shaping *how you endure.*

That's where resilience is built, not in grand, visible moments of triumph, but in the quiet decisions we make when no one's watching. That's the hidden gift of daily habits. They don't just track our progress; they create a baseline of strength that carries us through life's challenging moments.

THE 1 PERCENT BETTER EVERYDAY PHILOSOPHY

Daily practices are the foundation of building strong pillars, but consistency is what locks them in place. That's where the 1 Percent Better philosophy becomes essential. Knowing our pillars isn't enough; we need to strengthen them through small, consistent actions. Incremental growth turns our pillars from ideas into lived realities. Improving by just 1 percent each day is more than a productivity hack; it's the foundation of human growth and our overall evolution. While a 1 percent improvement might feel small in the moment, the cumulative effect over time is transformative. The magic of 1 Percent Better isn't in the size of the action; it's in the daily rhythm. When we fit this kind of improvement into our lives, we tend not to burn out, lose motivation, or give up. What I've learned is that small, incremental progress is different. It's sustainable. It doesn't rely on motivation, and it builds identity. (Remember, I became a runner starting with just one mile.)

When you improve by 1 percent every day, you're not just getting better at something; you're becoming someone different. James Clear put it perfectly: "Every action you take is a vote for the type of person you wish to become."[7] That's such a powerful concept. Think about it for a minute. We can become the people we want to be. We don't have to wait for something to happen to us. We just need to internalize consistent, incremental progress; no dramatic, unsustainable effort required. Whether it's working an extra hour on a project, writing a few more words, or spending a little more time with loved ones, every small improvement reinforces the identity of someone who shows up.

WHY 1 PERCENT WORKS

I didn't study biology in high school, and honestly, I wish I had. Understanding why things work helps me better internalize why I should do them. As I leaned more into living intentionally, my curiosity led me to wonder how habits form. From my own experience, I've discovered that the more we repeat something, the easier it becomes. Each repetition reinforces a path in my brain, much like carving a trail through the woods. That's why I can drop and do push-ups without hesitation; my brain already knows the way. What really surprised me is that this isn't just about biology; it's also about belief. When I stay consistent, I feel more grounded. My mind is clearer. I don't waste energy debating whether I'll show up; I just do. That's been the biggest shift: realizing that confidence and results don't stem from a spark of inspiration or some natural-born gift. It's something we build, one small, steady step at a time. The process of getting 1 percent better every day strengthens the pillars we've built:

- Improving by 1 percent is an act of **grit**—showing up even when you don't feel like it, pushing through discomfort and resistance.

- It's also an act of **grace**—recognizing that progress isn't always dramatic, but steady; trusting that small wins add up over time.

- And it's an act of **groundedness**—knowing that the path to growth is built on consistent effort, not fleeting motivation.

IDENTITY SHIFT: BECOMING 1 PERCENT BETTER

I've often thought about why people buy lottery tickets. For the record, I've never bought one. But it seems people want something to change their lives, like a big break or a wad of cash that will magically solve everything. The odds of winning the lottery are ridiculously low, but people keep buying tickets. What if we embraced the idea that we already have the winning ticket, and it's us? The way to cash it in isn't through luck; it's through daily practices and 1 Percent Better. We don't need a lottery win to change our lives; we just need to show up consistently and believe in our own agency.

Every time we complete an act, even in a small way, we reinforce the understanding that we are the kind of person who shows up, follows through, and keeps going. When we embrace this idea of our agency, we learn that:

- It's about becoming someone who values health.

- It's about becoming a writer.

- It's about becoming an entrepreneur.

Or whatever we want to be! The concept of 1 Percent Better is about becoming the person who lives the life we envision. Every small action strengthens our identity and reinforces the pillars we're building. That's how you cash in the winning ticket!

LEVERAGING YOUR PILLARS TO DESIGN YOUR INTENTIONAL LIFE

Living intentionally means consciously shaping how we live. It's about moving from passively reacting to life to actively designing it in alignment with our values, goals, and dreams. Designing our life means understanding what truly matters to us: the intersection of our aspirations, our strengths, and the impact we want to make. It's not about perfection; it's about clarity. When we know what we stand for and where we want to go, we stop drifting and start steering. This is where the G^3 pillars—grit, grace, and groundedness—become essential. Grit gives us the strength to keep going when things get hard. Grace reminds us to stay balanced and trust the process. Groundedness keeps us connected to our values, ensuring that we stay true to ourselves even as we evolve. Living intentionally isn't about having all the answers; it's about leveraging our pillars to make deliberate choices every day, shaping a life that reflects who we are and who we're becoming.

Now that we've explored the power of consistency and the pillars that sustain it, let's get practical. These steps are not meant to be rigid rules—they're a starting point. Use them to begin building a framework that supports your *why*, reinforces your habits, and helps you live with grit, grace, and groundedness every single day.

Step 1: Embrace Your Why

As we described in detail in Chapter 1, our *why* is the compass that guides every decision. It is the foundation that gives our life meaning. When we are clear on our *why*, we gain a powerful framework for making choices that align with our authentic selves. Ryan Holiday, a modern Stoic philosopher, emphasizes the importance of living in accordance with one's *why*. He suggests that true fulfillment arises from aligning actions with virtues such as courage, temperance, justice, and wisdom—the foundational principles of Stoicism. He believes that focusing on what we can control and practicing gratitude are essential components of a fulfilling life.[8]

As you define your *why*, reflect on these questions: "What brings you joy and fulfillment? What are the non-negotiables in your life? What principles have guided you during your most challenging times?"

Consider my co-worker Jenn: after the birth of her first child, she realized her *why* was family. She realigned her career and personal life to spend more time at home, even turning down promotions that didn't align with her goals. By defining her *why*, Jenn created a life focused on meaningful connections.

Step 2: Envision and Strengthen Your Pillars

Once you know your *why*, the next step is to envision the future you want to build. Your *why* shapes your pillars. When you know where you want to go, you can strengthen the habits and systems that will get you there. My good friend, Tom, spent years climbing the corporate ladder, but he always dreamed of something different. He envisioned opening a bike shop near the trail and helping others discover the joy of riding. It took courage and a loan, but he eventually made it happen. Running the shop hasn't been easy, but every time he sees someone riding because of his decision, he knows it was worth it.

Step 3: Design Your Environment

Your environment has a profound impact on your ability to live intentionally. The people you surround yourself with, the spaces you inhabit, and the routines you cultivate all shape your mindset and actions. Designing an environment that nurtures growth isn't just about aesthetics; it's about creating conditions that make success inevitable.

Kelly Sullivan Walden, my great friend, collaborator, and a ten-time author, inspirational coach, and speaker, embodies this principle. She knew that in order to live out her purpose, to inspire others through her writing, coaching, and speaking, she had to craft an environment that supported that vision. This meant not only curating a daily routine that prioritized creativity and mindfulness, but also surrounding herself with individuals who fueled her ambition, rather than draining it. She intentionally structured her life to align with her dreams, creating spaces that fostered deep thinking, engaging in rituals that kept her centered, and ensuring her daily interactions propelled her forward, rather than held her back. Kelly stands as a powerful example of intentional design in action. When we consciously shape our environment, we remove unnecessary friction, making it easier to stay aligned with our aspirations. The world around us either supports or sabotages our success; the key is choosing wisely.

Step 4: Reflect and Adjust

Life is dynamic, and so are we. Regular reflection ensures that your life-crafting efforts remain aligned with your evolving values and goals. Intentional living isn't about rigidly sticking to a plan; it's about continuously refining your approach. Ask yourself: "What's working well? Where am I facing resistance or frustration? What adjustments do I need to make to stay true to my vision?" Reflection sharpens our direction, but it's daily practices that carry us forward. Vision sets the destination, and consistent habits build the road.

Step 5: Build Daily Practices that Stick

The life you want is built one choice at a time. It's about consistency and small, intentional acts repeated with purpose. Daily practices are where our intentions become real. They serve as the invisible structure that shapes who we become. Here's how I've come to see it: we don't rise to the level of our goals; we fall to the level of our systems. I've trained for Ironman races, ultramarathons, and built businesses from the ground up. The common thread wasn't a superhuman trait; it was the daily rhythm: Wake up. Move. Fuel. Focus. Act. Reflect. Rest. Repeat.

To build practices that last, I follow these principles:

1. **Anchor in Purpose:** Every habit should point back to your *why*. If it doesn't, it won't stick.

2. **Make It Feel Possible:** Start where you are. Ten minutes is better than zero. A short walk today beats the perfect run you never take.

3. **Create Momentum:** Link new actions to existing ones. I journal right after my coffee. It's automatic because I pair it with something I already do.

4. **Honor the Ritual:** Treat your practice like a meeting with your future self. Show up even when it's hard, especially when it's hard.

5. **Track and Adjust:** Write it down (like in my spreadsheet). Reflect on how it's going. Celebrate what's working. Change what's not. This isn't about perfection; it's about persistence.

And when you miss a day? Grace. Don't allow one skipped practice to turn into a lost opportunity to start over. Intentional living isn't a one-time choice. The life you seek is being created in this moment, right now, through what you choose to do next.

So go ahead, set the alarm, lace up your shoes, write down the words, call your friend, and take the leap. Then, do it again tomorrow and fall in love with the process.

CHAPTER 3

EMBRACE THE CHALLENGE

Discomfort

Are we sorry for the feeling itself, or for how we feel about the feeling? Is it our nature to only seek comfort? Or are we created to endure, even embrace, discomfort? Our natural instinct seems to drive us toward the familiar, to stay where we feel safe. And yet, life does not appear to present itself that way. The moments we remember—the ones that define us—are rarely those spent in ease. They are the moments of struggle, challenge, and suffering. The times we were tested, stretched, and compelled to find something deeper within ourselves. Discomfort, though unwelcome, is where we grow. It's where we become. It seems paradoxical to say that discomfort is where the magic happens, but it is in the unfamiliar, the uncertain, and the difficult that we fully meet ourselves. In physical, emotional, and mental discomfort, we uncover our resilience, our clarity, our strength, and our meaning. Would we have discovered ourselves any other way?

WHY DISCOMFORT IS WHERE GROWTH HAPPENS

Discomfort is the hidden language of human potential. It speaks not in whispers, but in the raw, sometimes painful dialect of growth. Our bodies and minds have an extraordinary, often misunderstood mechanism: they don't just tolerate challenge, they require it. The first time I stepped into the world of ultra-marathons, I thought I knew everything about long-distance running. Thirty-five road marathons under my belt, and I believed I had mastered endurance. Then came my first fifty-mile trail race, a brutal awakening that redefined everything I thought I understood about my limits. Imagine transitioning from a four-hour road race to a ten-hour odyssey through unforgiving terrain. This wasn't just running anymore. This was a full-body negotiation with discomfort, limits, and the very concept of my potential.

The ultra running world welcomed me with a baptism of challenges: gut issues that fall into the TMI category, blisters that transformed my feet into masterpieces of suffering, chafing that felt like internal rebellion, and falls that reminded me how thin the line is between pushing limits and breaking completely. Maybe my relative ignorance was a blessing; I jumped in without overthinking and was forced to adapt in real time. Sixty ultras later, I've learned that challenge, discomfort, and suffering aren't obstacles: they're languages that teach resilience, adaptability, and the art of moving forward when everything screams to stop.

These lessons didn't remain confined to the trail. In my startup life, where I have served as the CEO of six early-stage companies and my teams have faced the strain of a delayed product launch or the gut punch of a slow sales quarter, I now approach challenges differently. The ultra mindset transformed me from a reactive leader into a calm, measured strategist. Where others see walls, I see negotiations. Where panic might rise, I view an opportunity to redistribute energy, accept what I'm dealt, and find a path forward. It's worked more often than not. Not because I was superhuman but because I learned to speak the language of discomfort, that is, to listen to its lessons and find strength in its whispers. Challenge doesn't break us; it reveals us.

To be clear, these ideas are not new; Stoic philosophers taught us to embrace suffering, not as an end, but as a pathway to resilience and wisdom. Marcus Aurelius, Roman emperor from 161 to 180 AD and a Stoic philosopher, once wrote, "What stands in the way becomes the way."[1] Similarly, Buddhist teachings remind us that suffering is not the enemy; it is a teacher. It's in learning to sit with discomfort, to face it without fear or resistance, that we transform pain into power.

The human mind and body make a remarkable interconnected system, finely tuned for survival and efficiency. To ensure stability and conserve energy lies a natural tendency toward homeostasis, a state of equilibrium. This was an essential adaptation when our ancestors faced scarce resources and constant threats. For early humans, preserving energy by maintaining balance often meant the difference between life and death. Resting, avoiding unnecessary risks, and conserving physical resources were survival strategies in a world of scarcity.

However, in today's world of climate-controlled rooms and Door-Dash deliveries, this same instinct can hold us back. We no longer need to hunt for food or guard against predators lurking outside the cave. Instead, we inhabit a world of abundance, where survival isn't the primary challenge. Our system still operates well in a state of minimal stress and maximal comfort. The problem is that homeostasis, while protective, doesn't push us to grow. It keeps us safe, but it also keeps us stagnant. In *The Comfort Crisis*, Michael Easter highlights how our modern pursuit of constant comfort can lead to a decline in our physical and mental resilience. He observes, "We are living progressively sheltered, sterile, temperature-controlled, overfed, under-challenged, safety-netted lives."[2] By constantly seeking comfort and avoiding challenges, we may inadvertently weaken our ability to adapt, grow, and thrive in the face of adversity.

Discomfort, then, is the mechanism by which we interrupt homeostasis and invite growth. When we encounter discomfort—be it physical, emotional, or psychological—we destabilize the system. The body and mind are forced to adapt, recalibrate, and evolve to meet the challenge. This process of destabilization triggers growth in ways that comfort never can.

THE SCIENCE OF DISCOMFORT AND GROWTH

Research in psychology and neuroscience supports this idea: growth happens outside the comfort zone. When we face challenges, our brain releases chemicals like adrenaline and dopamine, which heighten focus and motivation. Over time, repeated exposure to controlled stress, what psychologists call "eustress" or "good stress," helps us build resilience.[3] This is why practices like deliberate cold exposure, hot saunas, high-intensity exercise, or even public speaking can make us stronger over time. The key is finding the right combination: too little stress leads to stagnation, while too much can lead to burnout.

Consider how the body builds strength. When we lift weights, we create micro-tears in our muscle fibers. This is a form of controlled discomfort, where we deliberately push our body beyond its baseline capacity. In response, the body doesn't just repair the muscle; it rebuilds it stronger, preparing it for future challenges. Similarly, when we push ourselves mentally, we stretch our cognitive limits, creating new neural connections and expanding our ability to solve problems, manage stress, and achieve goals.

Moreover, discomfort activates the prefrontal cortex, the part of the brain responsible for decision-making and problem-solving. By stepping into discomfort, we're not just building emotional resilience; we're rewiring our brains to handle future challenges more effectively. Our dopamine system, the part of our brain that drives motivation and reward, thrives on challenge. Dopamine isn't just about pleasure; it's about pursuit. It propels us toward growth, fueling our desire to achieve more, learn more, and become better. But here's the catch: dopamine isn't activated when we stay in the safe zone of homeostasis. It lights up when we set a goal, take a risk, and push ourselves into the discomfort of the unknown.

This is why discomfort is essential for growth. It taps into the deepest mechanisms of human potential, overriding our instinct for comfort and compelling us to evolve. In the process, it rewires not just our muscles or our minds but our entire perspective. We begin to see discomfort not as something to avoid, but as a signpost pointing toward opportunity.

In January 2025, on his podcast, Rich Roll, known for his remarkable life transformation through endurance sports and plant-based living, had a very interesting conversation with performance expert Steve Magness, who offered a nuanced perspective on challenge and growth. Roll has consistently emphasized that true resilience isn't about suppressing emotions or displaying traditional toughness, but about thoughtfully engaging with discomfort. His shift from a struggling attorney to an ultra-endurance athlete exemplifies how confronting challenges can become a catalyst for profound personal transformation.

Unlike conventional narratives of grit that celebrate grinding through pain, Roll and Magness argue for a more holistic approach. It's not about how much you can endure, but how intelligently you can navigate and learn from challenging experiences. Their dialogue suggests that real growth happens not in the moment of maximum stress, but in our reflective response to that stress. That is how we process, integrate, and ultimately grow from difficult moments.[4]

I have come to appreciate the paradox of human adaptation. In comfort, we conserve. In discomfort, we transform. It's a delicate dance between preservation and evolution, where our systems are constantly recalibrating, always preparing for what comes next. In 2024, researchers Hermans et al., in *Biological Psychiatry*, made a profound observation: the acute stress response is a major driving force behind our adaptive capacity. Our bodies don't just endure stress; they learn from it, recalibrating and becoming more resilient with each challenge.[5]

My understanding of this principle crystallized during the 2022 Sea to Sea 300-mile adventure race, an odyssey that redefined my concept of endurance. Imagine seventy checkpoints stretched across Florida's most unforgiving terrain: a fifty-mile canoe segment, trails lined with razor-sharp palmetto slicing into our legs, and swamps so hot they seemed to drain every ounce of energy. Somewhere around fifty hours into the race, I realized something about discomfort: you can either resist it or negotiate with it. My racing partner, Dirk, and I quickly learned that survival meant finding micro-moments of comfort within the larger landscape of challenge: five minutes off our feet, a shared laugh, a breath that actually reached the bottom of our lungs, a candy bar pulled from a soggy backpack. These weren't signs of weakness; they were tactical resets. What fascinates scientists and athletes alike is how our bodies and minds respond to sustained stress. When pushed beyond familiar boundaries, we don't just endure, we recalibrate. Our muscles rebuild stronger, our neural pathways become more efficient, and our psychological resilience expands.

Our race resets weren't just practical survival tools; they revealed something deeper: that resilience isn't about white-knuckling our way through; it's about learning when to push and when to pause. What we found was this: growth isn't forged in constant struggle. It's born from the intelligent rhythm between effort and renewal. Too much comfort breeds complacency. Too much strain invites collapse. The magic lives in the in-between—in that sacred space where we willingly enter the fire of discomfort and then grant ourselves the grace of genuine rest, not just to recover, but to rebuild.

In adventure racing, as in life, we discovered that embracing discomfort isn't merely a tactic. It's a philosophy. We could have stayed home, safe on our couches. But instead, we stepped into the wild unknown. We tested our limits. We unearthed strength we didn't know we had. Every checkpoint became a reckoning. Every mile, a meditation. And at the finish line, after seventy sleepless hours, Dirk and I weren't just exhausted athletes, we were transformed humans, having redrawn the borders of what we once believed was possible.

Few stories capture the power of embracing discomfort quite like that of Diana Nyad, whose incredible feat of swimming from Cuba to Florida at the age of sixty-four redefined what it means to push human limits. The 110-mile open-water swim was not her first attempt. Over the years, she faced four failures and the "joy" of stinging jellyfish, hypothermia, exhaustion, and strong currents that repeatedly thwarted her dreams. Yet, she refused to quit. Her final attempt in 2013 was the culmination of over thirty years of perseverance. For more than fifty hours, Nyad endured excruciating physical pain, mental fatigue, and unpredictable seas. Every stroke was an act of defiance against doubt, discomfort, and the limits of what many believed was humanly possible. She emerged on the shores of Florida not just as a swimmer who had completed an epic journey, but as a symbol of resilience, determination, and the transformative power of discomfort.

I really like Nyad's "find a way" mantra as it became her guiding light through the darkness of challenges.[6] It's a reminder that growth isn't handed to us; it's earned through grit, through a willingness to lean into the discomfort that others might avoid. Her experience was not just a physical triumph; it was a mental and emotional challenge that showcased the strength we uncover when we embrace what is hard. She didn't just swim an ocean; she redefined what's possible when humans confront seemingly insurmountable obstacles. When I think about what Diana Nyad did, we all have an opportunity to be a version of her in our own lives. The "ocean" might look different for each of us: a career transition, a personal loss, a dream that seems just out of reach. The principle remains the same: growth happens at the edge of our comfort, in those moments when giving up feels easier than pushing through. I've learned this lesson in my own crucibles, particularly during ultra-endurance races where the line between possibility and impossibility blurs with each mile. My strategy isn't about suppressing discomfort but negotiating with it. At mile seventy-five of a hundred-mile race, when every muscle protests and the finish seems like a cruel mirage, I play a mental game that has become my own version of "find a way." I remind myself: This moment is temporary. In just a few days, I'll be sitting in my office, warm coffee in hand, and this discomfort will be nothing more than a memory, a badge of honor, a story of resilience. Time moves forward, with or without my consent. Each step, no matter how painful, is a step closer to something else. It's not about eliminating discomfort. It's about changing our relationship with it.

It is important that we recognize that not only will each of our "oceans" be different, but they will also change over time as we leverage our pillars and lean into living intentionally. At one point, it could be a personal goal that terrifies us. Later, it's a challenge that seems just beyond our reach. The specifics don't matter. What matters is that we have a continued willingness to step into the discomfort and to trust that we are more capable than we believe.

What would happen if you approached your own challenges with Nyad's spirit? If you saw discomfort not as a barrier, but as a bridge to your most authentic self? The journey of a thousand miles—or a hundred-mile race, or a 110-mile swim—begins with a single stroke, a single step. And sometimes, that step is the most courageous thing you'll ever do.

LEADVILLE TRAIL 100:
THE RACE THAT TESTED EVERYTHING

I'll never forget my first hundred-mile race, the Leadville Trail 100 in Colorado. A crucible of human endurance etched into the roof of the world. Committing to something you don't fully understand is a strange and thrilling process. I had completed a fifty-miler and a hundred-kilometer (sixty-two-mile) race, so stepping up to one hundred miles felt like a natural progression—just thirty-eight miles longer, right? The statistics were a gut punch: only 45 to 55 percent of runners finish Leadville, with half crossing the line in the final desperate hour before the cutoff. Thirty hours. That's all you get to prove yourself against the mountain. Miss a single aid station cutoff, and you're branded with the three most devastating letters in an endurance athlete's vocabulary: DNF (Did Not Finish).

The race begins at ten thousand feet, where the air is so thin it feels like breathing through a straw. The mountains don't just loom; they intimidate and challenge. Every step is a negotiation with gravity, your gut, and your breaking point. Hope Pass stands at 12,600 feet, a name dripping with bitter irony. You cross it twice, first at mile forty, then again at mile fifty-five. Each crossing is a battle against altitude, against your own doubt, against the voice that shouts you cannot continue.

From the first steps out of downtown Leadville, my watch became my tormentor. A thousand glances, each one a prayer, each one a fear, those aid station cutoffs ever present. Time stretched and contracted like some cruel elastic, bending to the mountain's will. As hours passed, the race revealed its true nature: this wasn't about speed; this was about survival. "Just make it to the next aid station" became my mantra. So what if my legs were screaming? So what if I'd crossed a thirty-four-degree stream (twice) that froze my bones? So what if gels had turned my stomach into a churning rebellion? Just keep moving.

Night brought its own special torment. Imagine running with nothing but the narrow beam of a headlamp, your world reduced to a tunnel of rocky trail and encroaching darkness. After eight hours, the tunnel of light became smaller and smaller. The trail blurred. The mountain whispered its challenge. It would be romantic to say I discovered some profound insight about human endurance. But the reality was far more primal. I was simply holding on. Battling blisters. Fighting exhaustion. Accepting discomfort as my only companion. No magical second wind. No divine intervention. Just the most basic, most powerful decision: keep going or stop.

After twenty-eight hours, I stumbled onto Sixth Street, the final stretch. The moment I crossed that finish line, I collapsed. Not in defeat but in triumph. I had not conquered the mountain. The mountain had transformed me. In the hours and days that followed, the race's true meaning crystallized. It wasn't about the finish line. It was about discovering the vast, unexplored territory of my own resilience. Could it be that it was not about the finish line, but about proving to myself that I could endure far more than I ever thought possible? When everything says stop, something inside can always say: one more step. This seems to be a good way to think about our path through life.

As I spend more and more time in the ultra-endurance community, I find more and more examples of seemingly regular people who are willing to push to their limits and beyond. A friend of mine, Elle, decided to climb Mount Kilimanjaro. She wasn't an experienced alpinist, but she wanted to prove to herself that she could rise to the challenge. The altitude, the cold, and the physical exhaustion tested her in ways she hadn't anticipated. Yet, standing at the summit, she said it was both the hardest and most rewarding experience of her life. She came down that mountain not just with a sense of accomplishment but with a renewed belief in her ability to face life's challenges head-on.

From my years of working through these challenges, I have adopted the mantra that "discomfort does not rise to the level of quit." We often quit far too early, allowing discomfort to overpower our resolve before we've truly tested our limits. Discomfort is an invitation to pause, reassess, and recalibrate, not a signal to stop altogether. The problem is that our instinctual reaction to discomfort often amplifies it. We feel the sting of difficulty and mistake it for an emergency, triggering a reflex to escape. But discomfort is rarely a valid reason to quit. It usually signals that we're standing at the edge of growth. Quitting prematurely robs us of the chance to adapt, to push beyond what feels possible, and to emerge stronger. The key lies in recognizing that discomfort, while uncomfortable, is temporary, and by pushing through resistance, true transformation happens.

> Discomfort is rarely a valid reason to quit. It usually signals that we're standing at the edge of growth. Quitting prematurely robs us of the chance to adapt, to push beyond what feels possible, and to emerge stronger. The key lies in recognizing that discomfort, while uncomfortable, is temporary, and by pushing through resistance, true transformation happens.

BREAKING THE HESITATION LOOP

Embracing discomfort isn't just a mindset, it's a practice. One of the biggest roadblocks we face isn't failure or fatigue. It's hesitation: that brief moment between instinct and action when our brain starts whispering all the reasons to wait, to pause, to stay safe. What we learn is that hesitation is the comfort zone's last line of defense. If we wait until we feel ready, we'll wait forever.

Mel Robbins, in her book *The 5 Second Rule*, offers a simple but powerful tool to combat hesitation and take action before fear and doubt take over. The rule is straightforward: the moment you feel the instinct to act, whether it's getting up early for a workout, speaking up in a meeting, or stepping into an uncomfortable challenge, you count down, "5-4-3-2-1," and move. No second-guessing. No allowing fear to creep in. Just action. This technique works because it short-circuits the brain's instinct to retreat into homeostasis: that comfortable, familiar state where we avoid risks and conserve energy. It interrupts the inner dialogue that so often convinces us to stay put, replacing overthinking with momentum. As Robbins explains, "There is a window for everyone between the moment you have an instinct to change and your mind killing that instinct." This is exactly why discomfort is so vital—it forces us out of autopilot and into growth. Whether it's pushing through fatigue in a race, making a difficult phone call, or embracing an unfamiliar opportunity, the 5 Second Rule provides a bridge between hesitation and action. It reminds us that we don't need to *feel* ready to start. We just need to move.[7]

Diana Nyad, in her relentless pursuit to swim from Cuba to Florida, embodied this same principle. Each stroke forward was a rejection of doubt, a decision to keep going despite the discomfort. Just like her mantra, "find a way," Robbins's 5 Second Rule reinforces that action, not overthinking, is the key to pushing past limits. When you find yourself hesitating, remember this: growth happens in the seconds between doubt and action. Count down and take the leap.

PRACTICAL STEPS TO GET COMFORTABLE WITH DISCOMFORT

Now that we understand the role of discomfort and how to move through hesitation, here are six ways to build a more intentional relationship with discomfort in your everyday life:

1. Reframe the Challenge

Instead of seeing discomfort as something to avoid, start viewing it as a gateway to growth. When discomfort arises, don't resist it; get curious. Ask yourself: "What is this trying to teach me? What strength can I develop through this experience?"

Action Step: The next time you feel uncomfortable, pause. Instead of withdrawing, sit with the feeling and ask: "What's the opportunity here?" Write it down.

2. Start Small (But Start!)

You don't have to dive into the deep end right away. Begin with small, controlled discomfort: a difficult workout, an honest conversation, or trying something new. Let success in small challenges build your confidence for larger ones.

Action Step: Pick one small challenge this week. Something that makes you a little uncomfortable. Write down how it made you feel and what you learned from it.

3. Practice Presence

Discomfort often comes from fear of the unknown. Anchor yourself in the present moment through mindfulness or breathwork. Presence helps reduce mental resistance and allows you to face discomfort calmly.

Action Step: When you feel discomfort, try a simple breathing exercise: Inhale for four counts, hold for four counts, exhale for four counts. Repeat until you feel more grounded.

4. Build a Support System

Surround yourself with people who will encourage you to push your limits but also hold you accountable. Growth is easier when you have a tribe that supports you through the hard moments.

Action Step: Identify one person in your life who can help hold you accountable. Share your goal with them and ask for their support.

5. Celebrate Progress

Growth isn't linear, and success doesn't come overnight. Celebrate the small wins along the way. It reinforces your progress and strengthens your motivation to keep going.

Action Step: At the end of each week, write down three things you did that pushed you out of your comfort zone and how they made you stronger.

6. Learn from Setbacks

When things go wrong, reflect on why and adjust your approach. Every setback is a lesson in disguise.

Action Step: After a setback, ask yourself: "What did I learn? What will I do differently next time?" Write it down.

WHY THIS MATTERS

Growth rarely announces itself with fanfare. It happens in quiet moments of choice, when we choose to stay in the difficult conversation, to push past the plateau, to face the challenge we have been avoiding. Embracing discomfort isn't about seeking pain or hardship for its own sake. It's about learning to navigate discomfort with grace and courage, and when we do, we unlock a deeper sense of purpose and capability. Remember: our body and mind are capable of far more than our comfort zone suggests. Every time we embrace discomfort, we are not just building physical or mental strength; we are expanding our understanding of what's possible and the richness of our potential. The next time discomfort arrives, welcome it as a teacher. It's not here to break you; it's here to show you who you can become.

CHAPTER 4

MASTERING REFLECTION

Daily Reflection

Some days fly by in a blur; others stretch out endlessly. Some days we give everything we have, while on other days we take a rare moment to breathe. But no matter the pace or the pressure, every day offers us something sacred, a chance to pause, to look back, and to ask ourselves: "Did I live today on purpose?" Daily reflection isn't about criticizing what went wrong or getting stuck in what could have been. It's about noticing—the life in our actions, the lessons in our struggles, the quiet moments that made us smile, and the integrity in our choices. It's a chance to recalibrate, not to judge; to check in, not check out. Did I live in alignment with my values? Did I speak with honesty, act with courage, and stay connected to my commitments? Reflection doesn't demand perfection; it simply asks for presence. It invites us to show up with honesty and an open heart. It reminds us that each day is a page in the story we are writing—a story we can revise, redirect, or recommit to at any moment. Daily reflection is the quiet practice that grounds us, grows us, and guides us toward the life we are intentionally building, one choice, one pause, one day at a time.

REFLECTION IS THE OPERATING SYSTEM FOR INTENTIONAL LIVING

I used to think reflection was a luxury, something for philosophers and poets, not for busy people trying to get through their day. I was wrong. The busier life gets, the more essential reflection becomes. It's the difference between moving forward and just moving. Intentional living is not about getting everything right; it's about mindfulness and awareness. It's about pausing long enough to ask: "Who am I? What am I doing? Why does this matter?" In a world that is noisy, demanding, and distracting, reflection is how we stop and recalibrate. Reflection is like adjusting our sails mid-course. Without it, we can drift aimlessly. With it, we can correct our course, align with the wind, and move toward our destination with purpose.

The practice of reflection is as old as human civilization itself. Ancient philosophers, spiritual leaders, and scholars have long emphasized its role in personal growth and self-awareness. Socrates, often referred to as the father of Western philosophy, famously proclaimed, "The unexamined life is not worth living."[1] This idea, that reflection is necessary to live a meaningful and intentional life, laid the foundation for centuries of thought about self-assessment and introspection.

In Eastern traditions, practices such as meditation and mindfulness have been used for thousands of years to cultivate awareness and clarity.

Buddhist teachings emphasize the importance of observing one's thoughts and actions without judgment, a practice that allows individuals to gain insight into their own minds and behaviors. It's about creating small moments of clarity every day. Similarly, in Stoicism, reflection plays a critical role in understanding one's values and aligning actions with purpose. Marcus Aurelius, in his *Meditations*, provides a powerful example of daily reflection. His writings were not intended for publication but as a personal practice to examine his thoughts, behaviors, and growth.[2]

As history progressed, reflection evolved into structured practices. Journaling became a tool for writers, thinkers, and leaders to record their experiences and make sense of their lives. Visionaries like Leonardo da Vinci, Ralph Waldo Emerson, and Virginia Woolf used writing as a form of self-discovery, leaving behind not only a record of their thoughts but also a roadmap for how reflection fuels creativity and clarity.

In recent decades, reflection has gained renewed attention as a cornerstone of intentional living. The fast pace of modern life has left so many people feeling disconnected from themselves, their goals, and their values. In response, practices like mindfulness, journaling, and gratitude have emerged as essential tools for cultivating meaning, clarity, and purpose. Leaders in business, education, and wellness are now encouraging reflection as a daily habit, recognizing its profound impact on decision-making, emotional well-being, and long-term growth. Melanie Perkins, cofounder and CEO of Canva, credits her morning reflection practice as crucial to scaling her company from a small startup to a forty-billion-dollar juggernaut. "I love reading tweets from our Canva community and have just started using the *Five Minute Journal*...," she shared in a questionnaire, "It's a lovely way to start the day and helps to ensure I'm proactively shaping my day ahead."[3] This quiet time, filled with gratitude and reflection, helps her stay grounded in Canva's mission, even when things get chaotic. Today, reflection is not limited to philosophers or spiritual leaders. It has become a practical, accessible tool for anyone seeking to live with intention. Technology has even begun to play a role in how we reflect, from apps that guide mindfulness and gratitude to journaling and wearable devices that track physical and emotional states. More people than ever are beginning to integrate moments of pause into their lives, discovering that even small moments of reflection can yield significant insights and transformation.

Many contemporary thought leaders have embraced reflection as an essential practice. Gretchen Rubin, author of *The Happiness Project* and cohost of the *Happier* podcast, emphasizes the power of self-reflection in shaping habits and happiness. Her work highlights how understanding our tendencies, why we do what we do, can help us design lives that align with our values and goals. Through her discussions, Rubin provides strategies to integrate reflection into daily routines, making intentional living more accessible and sustainable.[4] Likewise, Kelly Berry, host of the *Life Intended* podcast, champions self-reflection as a tool for personal growth. In her solo episode, "10 Questions for a More Intentional Life," she encourages listeners to ask themselves deep, introspective questions that reconnect them with their authentic selves. Berry's approach illustrates that reflection isn't just about looking back; it's about actively shaping the path ahead through greater clarity and self-awareness.[5]

For most of my adult working life, being by myself terrified me, and reflection was something that happened in a mirror. I was the person always seeking external validation, always chasing the next conversation, the next opportunity. Business trips meant organizing group dinners. The thought of spending an evening alone in a hotel room felt like a form of punishment. What could possibly happen in that silent space? Who would validate my worth if I weren't constantly surrounded by others? Looking back, I realize I was running from myself. Afraid of the quiet. Afraid of the questions that might emerge if I stopped long enough to listen. Reflection found its way into my life unexpectedly with an Ironman race rule that changed everything: no headphones allowed. Suddenly, my training runs became a confrontation with my own thoughts. No music. No podcasts. No escape. Just miles of uninterrupted internal dialogue. At first, it was challenging. My mind bounced like a pinball, desperate for distraction. But slowly, something remarkable happened. The noise began to settle. The chaos transformed into clarity. Running became my unexpected sanctuary of reflection. What started as a physical necessity evolved into a daily ritual of internal exploration. Each mile became a conversation with myself, working through team challenges, processing investor meetings, and dreaming up new adventures. My daily run was no longer just exercise; it became a two-for-one investment in both physical and mental growth.

Thousands of miles later, I've learned that reflection isn't about having all the answers. It's about creating space to ask better questions. It's about giving yourself permission to sit with uncertainty, to explore your thoughts without judgment. Running isn't a universal solution. Not everyone finds their reflection on miles of pavement or trail. But everyone can find their own method, such as yoga, meditation, walking, or journaling. The medium matters less than the commitment. All you need are your thoughts, a few intentional questions, and the courage to listen. The world will always have noise. Reflection is the art of finding the signal within the noise.

As I learned, at its core, reflection is the practice of self-assessment. It allows us to process our experiences, thoughts, and emotions, and then use those insights to adjust our actions. It's how we ensure that we are not living on autopilot, but moving with intention toward our goals, values, and purpose. Without reflection, we risk drifting, staying in familiar patterns, and reacting to life instead of directing it. Think of reflection as the bridge between experience and growth. Life constantly hands us opportunities to learn from our successes, failures, relationships, and challenges. But growth doesn't happen automatically. It happens when we embrace and heighten our awareness of what is going on in our lives, reflect on our experiences, extract the requisite lessons, and apply them moving forward.

For all of us seeking to live intentionally, reflection is not a luxury; it's a necessity. It's how we identify what's working and what isn't. It's how we clarify what matters most. And it's how we ensure that our actions align with the life we want to create. Over time, I've noticed something fascinating: when I pause to reflect, really pause, my thinking shifts. It's as if my mind steps away from the noise, and the aperture opens wider. Patterns emerge. Clarity returns. I see connections I would have missed if I'd remained buried in task mode. That space, quiet, expansive, and honest, gives me the perspective I need to navigate life's challenges with greater vitality, resilience, and purpose. That's what reflection builds: a platform to stand on, not just for ourselves, but for the people we serve and support.

> For all of us seeking to live intentionally, reflection is not a luxury; it's a necessity. It's how we identify what's working and what isn't. It's how we clarify what matters most. And it's how we ensure that our actions align with the life we want to create.

REFLECTION WORKS AT DIFFERENT LEVELS

Reflection is not a single instrument, but an entire orchestra, capable of playing both delicate daily melodies and sweeping lifetime symphonies. We navigate life using two critical lenses of reflection: the micro daily adjustments and the macro life-defining insights. Understanding how to use both micro and macro reflections gives us the ability to steer our lives with more precision and purpose. Micro-reflection helps with fine-tuning the daily execution, while macro-reflection ensures that we are headed in the right long-term direction.

Ray Dalio, the legendary investor and author, built his entire business and life philosophy around this principle of balancing short-term adjustments with long-term strategy. His book, *Principles,* is essentially a playbook on how to use reflection to drive better decision-making. Dalio frames life as a continuous feedback loop: make decisions, then reflect on outcomes, where necessary, adjust, and then make better decisions.[6] Reflection isn't just about processing the past; it's about upgrading how we operate in the future.

REFLECTION ISN'T ALWAYS A SOLO ACT

Sometimes the most powerful insights come from the outside looking in. Feedback from colleagues, friends, or family acts as an emotional mirror, showing us what we might miss when we're too close to the situation. Feedback helps shift our processing from the reactive amygdala (the emotional part of the brain) to the strategic prefrontal cortex (the logical, decision-making part). When we feel defensive, that's often a sign that reflection is most needed. If we can step back and view feedback not as criticism but as data, we unlock the ability to reflect more objectively and make sharper decisions.

WHEN FEEDBACK FORCED ME TO REFLECT

I experienced this shift during my time at Ernst & Young. The path to make partner was brutal—seventy-hour weeks, constant travel, and cutthroat competition. I had risen quickly from manager to senior manager, producing great results, building a strong team, and earning stellar client reviews. I was up for the role of partner, and I was certain I'd be selected.

I didn't get selected.

The rejection felt like a personal indictment. I came home defeated, collapsing onto a chair, disappointment seeping into my bones. Anthea walked in, saw my state, and instead of offering sympathy, she dropped a verbal gauntlet: "If you want this so badly, why don't you prove them wrong?" I protested. It was a year away, and they should have picked me now. But Anthea wasn't budging. "Kiddo, if this really matters to you, then make it happen." She walked away to tend to the girls. Her words weren't a platitude; they were a call to action. In that moment, I had a choice. I could wallow in rejection or use it as a strategic pause. Anthea's intervention shifted me from a reactive, emotional state to a strategic, reflective mindset. I began dissecting my performance and approach. My certainty had blinded me to areas for potential improvement. Over the next year, I reflected both on the big picture and the finer details, what I was doing well and where I needed to improve. I built a deliberate plan, focusing not on proving the selection committee wrong but on becoming unquestionably the right candidate for the role. Twelve months later, I was unanimously selected as a partner, one of the youngest to make the role.

That experience taught me that reflection isn't just about processing failure; it's about converting setbacks into strategy. Feedback from others can feel uncomfortable, but when we view it as an opportunity instead of a threat, it becomes one of the most powerful tools for growth. That shift, from the reactive to the strategic, became the foundation of how I've approached every challenge since. It built a muscle I've leaned on ever since, a muscle that keeps me performing at my peak. Reflection became my edge, transforming disappointment into clarity and setbacks into springboards for future success.

THE SCIENCE OF REFLECTION

While we acknowledge that the idea of reflection has been around for over two thousand years, it is reinforcing to see that studies in cognitive science reveal why reflection is more than just self-help advice:

- A 2014 study at Harvard Business School found that employees who spent fifteen minutes reflecting at the end of their workday showed a 23 percent improvement in job performance over those who didn't.[7]

- Neuroscience research using fMRI scans showed that reflection activated the default mode network (DMN) in our brains—the same network associated with recall, emotional processing, and personal meaning-making.[8]

- In a *Harvard Business Review* article, "Why Leaders Don't Learn From Success," they found that students who reflected on their experiences showed a significantly better learning rate compared to those who accumulated experience without reflection.[9]

Growth doesn't occur by remaining comfortable. It happens when we intentionally step into the unknown, confront challenges, and push past the edge of what feels easy or familiar. Our bodies and minds are wired for stability; we're designed to seek comfort and conserve energy. This made sense when survival was our primary concern. However, in today's world, where most of us aren't fighting off predators or braving the wilderness, this instinctual tendency to avoid discomfort can hinder us from realizing our potential. Discomfort disrupts that stability. It compels us to adapt, stretch, and grow. It triggers the very systems in our brain and body that ignite motivation, focus, and transformation. Whether we're lifting weights, tackling a complex issue, or engaging in a tough conversation, stepping into discomfort unleashes a chain reaction that fosters mental, physical, and emotional strength. That's why discomfort isn't something to fear; it's a signal that we're moving in the right direction. Every time we push through what's challenging, we increase our capacity, not just to do more, but to become more.

BUILDING A DAILY REFLECTION PRACTICE

Reflection isn't passive; it's a performance tool. Whether it's daily micro adjustments or long-term macro recalibrations, reflection allows us to align our actions with our goals. And sometimes the most valuable reflection comes from the outside looking in. The good news is that a reflection practice doesn't need to be complicated, but it does need to be consistent. Daily reflection provides a rhythm, a regular pause to check in with ourselves, process our day, and realign with our goals. Reflection takes many forms, and the approach we choose can depend on what feels most natural to us. These methods are not only tools for processing our day but also practices for deepening our self-awareness and building intentional habits over time.

Carve Out Time: Take five to ten minutes for a morning reflection and before checking your phone, ask yourself:

- What's one thing I want to feel today?

- What's one thing I want to accomplish?

- How do I want to show up today?

Ask the Right Questions: The quality of our reflection depends on the questions we ask. Here are a few to get you started:

- What am I grateful for today?

- What challenges did I face, and how did I respond?

- Did my actions align with my values and priorities?

- What can I do differently tomorrow?

Write It Down: Journaling is one of the most powerful tools for reflection. Writing helps us slow down, organize our thoughts, and uncover insights we might miss otherwise. Your journal doesn't have to be perfect since it's not about writing for anyone else. It's about creating a space where you can be honest with yourself.

TOOLS FOR REFLECTION

Meditation: Meditation is one of the oldest and most powerful practices for reflection. Rooted in ancient traditions, meditation trains us to slow down, observe our thoughts without judgment, and find clarity in the present moment.

- *Why it works*: By creating space for stillness, meditation allows us to detach from the noise of daily life and listen to our inner voice.

- *How to start*: Begin with five to ten minutes of guided meditation or silent breathing. Focus on your breath, let your thoughts come and go, and observe where your mind naturally drifts.

Tip: Apps like Calm or Headspace offer accessible ways to integrate meditation into your routine.

Breathwork: Breathwork is the intentional practice of controlling our breathing to regulate our mind and body. It can be a powerful gateway into reflection, as focused breathing helps center our thoughts and calm our nervous system.

- *Why it works*: Our breath connects our mind and body. Intentional breathwork can help release stress, improve focus, and set the stage for deeper introspection.

- *How to start*: Try box breathing. Inhale for four counts, hold for four counts, exhale for four counts, and pause for four counts. Repeat for a few minutes.

Tip: Incorporate breathwork before journaling or meditating to create mental space for reflection.

Time Alone: In a constantly connected world, solitude is a rare and underrated form of reflection. Quiet time spent alone, without distractions, gives us the space to process our experiences, think creatively, and reconnect with our purpose.

- *Why it works*: Solitude quiets external influences, allowing us to think more deeply and honestly.

- *How to start*: Schedule small pockets of time each week for intentional solitude. Take a walk, sit in a quiet space, or simply turn off all screens and distractions.

  Tip: Use this time to ask yourself meaningful questions: "What do I need right now? What am I learning? What do I value most?"

Journaling: Writing is a structured and accessible way to reflect. By putting our thoughts onto paper, we externalize what might otherwise remain scattered in our minds. Journaling helps us organize, process, and make sense of our experiences.

- *Why it works*: Writing creates clarity. It allows us to see patterns, track progress, and capture insights that might otherwise be forgotten.

- *How to start*: Start with a few sentences at the end of the day. Reflect on what happened, how you felt, and what you learned.

  Tip: Use prompts to guide your writing. Questions like: "What am I proud of today? What challenged me? What can I improve tomorrow?" These are great starting points.

Time in Nature: Nature has a unique way of clearing mental clutter and offering perspective. Stepping away from the busyness of life and immersing ourselves in natural surroundings can serve as a powerful form of reflection.

- *Why it works*: Being in nature reduces stress, calms the mind, and fosters a sense of connection to something larger than ourselves. It creates a space for deeper thinking and awareness.

- *How to start*: Take a walk in a park, hike a trail, or simply sit outdoors in a quiet, natural setting. Pay attention to the sights, sounds, and sensations around you.

Tip: Use your time in nature to focus on a single question or topic. Let the rhythm of walking or the stillness of sitting guide your thoughts.

Mindfulness: Mindfulness is the practice of being fully present in the moment. When we pause and observe our thoughts without judgment, we create space for clarity. Mindfulness can amplify our reflection practice by helping us stay grounded and aware.

- *Why it works*: Mindfulness helps us stay present as we process past events. It allows us to notice recurring thoughts or patterns that need our attention and approach our experiences with curiosity rather than criticism.

- *How to start*: Try a simple mindfulness exercise before reflection. Take three to five deep breaths, focusing on your inhale and exhale. Notice any thoughts or feelings that arise and let them come and go without attaching to them.

Tip: Practice mindfulness during everyday activities, like washing dishes or walking, to make it a natural part of your day.

Gratitude Lists: Gratitude is one of the simplest yet most profound tools for reflection. By shifting our focus to what's good, even on hard days, we reframe our perspective and build resilience.

- *Why it works*: Gratitude helps us recognize the positives in our lives, fostering a sense of abundance and reducing negative thinking. It builds emotional resilience by training our brain to focus on what's working.

- *How to start*: Write down three to five things you're grateful for each day. They can be big (a supportive friend) or small (a warm cup of coffee). Be specific and reflect on why each thing matters to you.

Tip: If you're feeling stuck, try focusing on different areas of life—relationships, health, career, or personal growth—to uncover overlooked sources of gratitude.

YOUR INNER COMPASS

Reflection is your compass for intentional living. It's how we learn, how we grow, and how we ensure our days don't slip by unnoticed. It's how we align our actions with our purpose, so we move through life not just doing but becoming. When we build a habit of reflection, its ripple touches everything: greater clarity in our goals, more confidence in our decisions, and more profound gratitude for how far we've come. Most of all, it allows us to show up each day with greater awareness and intention. Reflection is a practice, not a destination. Like any skill, it deepens with time. Start where you are. Use what works. Let your practice evolve as you do. And trust that it's working, even when the insights come slowly. Pay attention not just to the answers, but to the questions that begin to rise. Notice how your awareness sharpens, how your understanding expands, how your inner voice begins to guide you more clearly.

So, take a moment. Be still.
Ask the questions. Trust what comes.

Because everything you're seeking?

It's already within you.

CHAPTER 5

FROM FAILURE TO FUEL

The Alchemy of Adversity

Adversity is nature's teacher, a masterful alchemist that transforms minerals into gold, weakness into strength, and defeat into possibility. It arrives unannounced, uninvited, wearing the mask of failure but carrying the blueprint of transformation. What tests us most is not the obstacle itself but our response to it. In moments of profound challenge, we discover a version of ourselves hidden beneath layers of comfort and predictability. We are not defined by what happens to us but by what we do with what happens to us. Resilience is not a trait we're born with; it's a muscle we build through repeated confrontation with discomfort. Each setback is an invitation: Will we crumble, or will we create? With practice, doubt becomes the raw material for confidence. Fear becomes the spark of courage. Failure is not an endpoint but a launching pad. The most powerful stories of human achievement are not tales of effortless success but narratives of persistent reinvention.

They are written in the language of struggle, translated through unwavering determination. Adversity isn't the enemy. It's the mentor we didn't ask for but often need most. It pushes us to the edge of what we believe is possible and then dares us to go further. It doesn't just test our limits; it redraws them.

WHEN FAILURE BECOMES YOUR SUPERPOWER

You're going to fail. Often and spectacularly. We've all been there, frozen by the fear of failure, so we either don't start or play it so safe we might as well not have tried. The word "failure" carries a weight that can feel unbearable. In a society that celebrates success and idealizes perfection, failure is framed as something to be feared, avoided, or even hidden. But what if failure wasn't an ending at all? What if it were an essential waypoint on the path to growth and fulfillment? Here's the thing about failure that nobody tells you: the people who succeed the most are usually the ones who've failed the most spectacularly.

Failure is not the opposite of success; it's the foundation of it. It's not a roadblock but a bridge. It's a passageway that grants us wisdom, resilience, and perspective. Every great innovator, athlete, and leader has learned to reframe failure as fuel. It's what propels them forward. When we stop seeing failure as a verdict and start seeing it as a teacher, we strip it of its power to shame. We harness it as a force that drives us toward mastery. Failure, when embraced, becomes the momentum we need to rise higher, stronger, and wiser.

In a conversation with Steven Bartlett on *The Diary of a CEO* podcast in 2025, author Robert Greene delved into the concept of failure and its integral role in achieving mastery. Greene emphasized that viewing failure as a natural and essential part of the learning process allows individuals to embrace challenges and persist through setbacks. He suggests that by accepting failure, we can transform it into a powerful tool for personal development.[1]

Organizational psychologist Adam Grant offers a nuanced view of failure, highlighting the subjective nature of many of our perceived shortcomings. In his discussion with actor and writer David Duchovny on the *WorkLife* podcast, Grant points out that often, failures relate to self-imposed expectations rather than objective standards. He advocates for redefining our goals and understands that falling short can be a valuable part of the growth process.[2] By integrating these perspectives, we can shift our mindset to see failure not as a definitive end but as a stepping stone toward resilience, wisdom, and ultimately, success.

So, should we believe the definition of failure in Webster's dictionary or the practical reality of our lived experiences? As the existential psychiatrist Irvin D. Yalom once said, "Sooner or later she had to give up the hope for a better past."[3] That single idea holds tremendous power. We can't rewrite what happened, but we can reshape how we carry it. What we call failure often lingers because we keep revisiting it with regret, hoping it turns out differently. But the moment we accept the past as unchangeable, we free up energy to shape what's still in our control—the present and everything beyond it. Failure is simply the opportunity to grow, and the more we embrace this fundamental reality, the better life becomes.

THE BISON EFFECT: WHY SOME PEOPLE GET STRONGER UNDER PRESSURE

There's a reason I have three bison tattooed on my arm. It's more than just ink; it's a daily reminder of resilience inspired by a piece of art originally painted by my daughter, Julianne. Bison are unique animals that have long symbolized strength, freedom, and endurance. When faced with a storm, most animals instinctively run away or try to avoid it. But bison? They lower their heads and charge straight into it. It's neither bravado nor stubbornness; it's a strategy. By facing the storm head-on, they spend less time in it. The same storm that might chase them for hours if they ran away passes over them quickly when they confront it directly. Bison live in harmony with their surroundings but remain unyielding in the face of obstacles, offering a powerful lesson in cultivating resilience in our own lives.

Living intentionally means embracing life's challenges with the same quiet strength as the bison. It means standing firm in our values, leading with integrity, pushing through discomfort, and trusting that the storms we face will shape us into stronger people. I think about this every time I face a challenge that feels overwhelming. Whether it's launching a new business venture, tackling an ultramarathon, or navigating a personal setback, the bison remind me: lower your head, lean into the wind, and keep moving forward. That's how resilience is built, and that's how we grow.

LET'S THINK DIFFERENTLY ABOUT FAILURE

For centuries, failure has been framed as a definitive end. In school, a failing grade meant you didn't pass. In workplaces, failure could cost a promotion or even a job. Culturally, failure became synonymous with inadequacy, leading many of us to internalize the belief that failing marked the limit of our potential. This mindset was reinforced by societal pressures to "get it right" and avoid mistakes at all costs.

But failure isn't always about results. Often, it's about mindset. Many people are physically and intellectually capable of breakthroughs, but without the right beliefs, tools, or feedback, they stay stuck.

Roger Bannister breaking the four-minute mile serves as the perfect example. He didn't suddenly become faster; he finally had the conditions to measure and refine his effort—timekeeping, training support, and inner belief. On May 6, 1954, at Oxford, he ran 3:59.4 and shattered a barrier many believed was humanly impossible. Just forty-six days later, Australian runner John Landy broke it too, running 3:57.9. That moment was proof: it wasn't just about ability—it was about belief. One man demonstrated it could be done, and suddenly the floodgates opened. Over the next few years, more runners joined them under four minutes, and today, more than 1,700 have achieved it. The limits had always existed physically, but once the mental barrier cracked, momentum carried the rest. That's the power of mindset. And it's also the power of community. Bannister didn't do it alone—he trained with friends who believed in him, paced him, and supported him when the world said it couldn't be done.

This evolving understanding of failure and capability has reshaped how we think about progress. The rapid pace of innovation, entrepreneurship, and personal development has shown us that failure is not an endpoint but a necessary part of growth. Groundbreaking ideas often emerge from countless trials, and success stories are built on perseverance and resilience. The framing of failure has shifted from a judgment of worth to a testament of adaptability and learning.

The startup community in the United States is a truly unique environment that has evolved and blossomed into a business community that fosters new thinking, creativity, business breakthroughs, and opportunity in ways that no other country has mastered quite as well. What we see in the prototypical startup failure is a deep level of learning, new technical models, and new business models that previously had not been tried. While they might not "make it" in their first attempt, they often become the seed of another startup sometime in the future. The multiple startup founder is revered and sought after for new ventures because they have the "right stuff" to work through the uncertainty of a new business, and bring the experience of what worked and what did not work, as well as the confidence that if it does not work, they will be fine. In the early days of Silicon Valley, the acceptance of "failure" seemed crazy, but it truly has become the lifeblood of American innovation, especially in the tech space.

After almost twenty years of working in large organizations, I had my first opportunity to lead a startup as CEO. We focused on bringing innovative ordering solutions to quick-serve and fast-casual restaurants, building remote-operated call centers for drive-thru throughput operations and online ordering (lunch, catering, etc.) on an iPad from 2006 to 2009. We rolled out a great deal of tech innovation and achieved some success with early adopters. However, we were too early to market. Franchise operators and consumers seemed satisfied with the fax and phone systems of the time, and we never quite hit our glide path to significant growth. Years later, none of us would imagine sending a fax order for lunch, but what I gained from this "failure" set me up to run my next company, and the one after that, and again and again. Now, having served as CEO of six startups, with a success rate of three out of six, I feel great about the process and the struggle, what I learned, and how it enabled me to tackle each successive startup adventure.

While on the surface, it seems that this new kind of perspective might not work for everyone, it is surely a way to view failure not as an indictment of our abilities but as evidence of our willingness to take risks, push boundaries, and embrace feedback loops that lead to improvement. It opens the door to a more empowering narrative in business and life. One that celebrates learning, adaptability, and the courage to try again.

GLOBAL PERSPECTIVES ON FAILURE

We can also learn from how people abroad deal with failure and see that threads all around the world are creating an international culture of success through failure—a very encouraging direction for all of us.

The Japanese Concept of Kaizen

In Japan, failure isn't seen as an event but as part of a continuous improvement process. The concept of *kaizen* teaches that small failures are essential feedback mechanisms. This is why Japanese manufacturers encourage workers to stop production lines when they spot potential issues, a practice that initially seemed counterintuitive to Western businesses.

German Failure Management

German business culture approaches failure with characteristic precision. They've even coined the term *Fehlerkultur* (failure culture), emphasizing systematic analysis over emotional response. German companies often maintain detailed "failure logs" to ensure the same mistakes aren't repeated.

Indigenous Wisdom on Failure

Many Indigenous cultures view failure not as a personal shortcoming but as a natural part of the community's learning process. The Navajo concept of *hózhó* teaches that imbalance (including failure) is as natural as balance, and both are necessary for growth.

The Nordic Educational Approach

Finnish schools, consistently ranked among the world's best, have nearly eliminated the concept of academic failure. Instead, they use a "failure-positive" approach where mistakes are treated as expected parts of the learning process. This has resulted in higher student engagement and better overall outcomes.

The African Ubuntu Philosophy

The concept of *ubuntu* (I am because we are) transforms failure from an individual burden into a collective learning opportunity. This communal approach to handling setbacks has proven particularly effective in building resilient communities and businesses across Africa.

THE LANGUAGE OF POTENTIAL

Words shape how we experience the world. They're not just descriptions—they're directions. When we reframe how we talk about setbacks, we begin to unlock new ways to grow through them. I learned this firsthand during my time at Mainspring. We were on a rocket ride—an eighteen-month growth spurt—and preparing to go public when the Nasdaq dropped six hundred points in just days. The IPO was in jeopardy. But instead of seeing it as a failure, we chose to reframe it as a chance to refocus and strengthen the business. That simple shift, from disaster to opportunity, reshaped our thinking. When we relaunched, the IPO went even better than expected. We didn't just survive the setback; we grew through it.

Try this: notice how you talk about the moments that don't go as planned. Swap "failure" for "feedback" and "mistake" for "lesson." Small shifts in language lead to big shifts in belief. And belief? That's where growth begins.

FAILURE AS FUEL

When we think of failure, we often see it as the end, a signal that we've hit a wall, proven our limits, or fallen short. But what if failure is the clearest sign that we're pushing the edge of what we're capable of? What if it's not a verdict, but a marker of boldness?

Sara Blakely, founder of Spanx, credits her father with transforming how she viewed failure. "So, I would come home from school and [my dad] would say to my brother and me 'So, what'd you guys fail at this week?' And if I didn't have something, he would actually be disappointed.... He was just changing my definition of failure. My definition of failure became not about the outcome, but about not trying." she said in an interview. Her mindset helped her build a billion-dollar brand.[4]

What we learn is that success is often built on the ashes of failed attempts. Every rejection, misstep, or false start is evidence that you're in the arena, doing the work. The key is not to avoid failure, but to extract the lesson, make the adjustment, and keep going. What sets successful people apart isn't that they never fall. It's that they get back up, smarter, stronger, and more determined.

LOVING THE EDGE

When we shift our mindset to embrace failure, we begin to see the edges of our capabilities as exciting, not terrifying. The edge is where we test our limits, stretch beyond what we thought possible, and uncover our true potential. It is where we are close to failure, but not at the breakpoint. It comes in different "flavors," like discomfort or annoyance. This is something I've learned deeply as an ultramarathon runner. After hundreds of training sessions and countless races, I know the edge isn't theoretical; it's real, visceral, and often brutal. Toward the end of a hundred-mile race, when my legs feel like lead, my breathing is ragged, and I just feel uncomfortable, it seems like quitting is the only logical choice. But here's the thing: that's exactly when I know I'm about to break through. I start by reconnecting to my *why*. I remind myself that I am not here by accident. This was intentional. I knew what I was getting myself into and the discomfort that would come. It calms my nervous system, and I am reminded that discomfort is not a signal to quit; it's the gateway to growth. I can listen to the pain or push beyond it. And every time I lean into that edge, something shifts. My legs are still burning, my lungs are still on fire, but my mind grows sharper, my focus steadier. That's where the magic happens. It is where new limits are forged. But this isn't just about running. The edge exists in every area of life. It's the hard conversation you've been avoiding, the business risk you've been hesitating to take, the creative project you're scared to put into the world. Learning to love the edge means embracing that discomfort, not as a threat, but as proof that you're growing. The edge is where transformation happens. And when you realize you can survive the edge, you stop fearing it. That's when you start to feel unstoppable.

THE DNF AND WHAT IT TAUGHT ME

I remember standing in the mountains south of Tucson, soaked to the bone, shivering uncontrollably. It was 34 degrees with driving rain and 50 mph winds, and I was completely lost. My first big race, a fifty-miler, had gone from excitement to survival. Now, here I was, about to become another statistic.

The race started well. For the first twenty miles, I felt strong and confident. But then I saw the sky darkening to the west. A spring monsoon was rolling in fast. The temperature had dropped into the thirties, the wind was picking up, and freezing rain began pelting me. I told myself it would pass. It didn't. I was dressed in nothing but a T-shirt, shorts, and a light jacket—completely unprepared for the storm. The course markings were blown away, and I made a wrong turn. Before I knew it, I was lost in the mountains. I wandered for ten miles. Every tree looked the same and I was feeling a deep level of panic. My legs were cramping, my breathing was shallow, and the cold was cutting through me. Hypothermia was setting in. I could not decide if I should just sit there or keep moving. It was not looking promising. Just when I thought I was done, I saw movement, a National Guardsman out looking for lost runners was on the other side of the trail. I faintly called out. I called out again. It took a few more efforts and, thankfully, he heard me. I could barely explain how bad I felt, but he told me to sit down while he ran to get help. The medics arrived thirty minutes later with wool blankets, hot tea, and supportive words. My legs were seizing up, but with their help, I made it to the aid station soon to be on the list of DNFs.

I was just a few miles from safety, but in those conditions, it might as well have been a hundred. Sitting in the aid station, the shame started sinking in. My mind was racing. How was I going to write my blog and tell everyone that I didn't finish? That I failed? That I wasn't the tough guy I portrayed myself to be? My identity at risk, I struggled with the mental anguish as much as the bone-chilling cold that had overtaken me. I had to wait for what seemed like forever for my buddy, Joe D., to finish the race, and as I waited, I kept spiraling. No one in the aid station knew how I was feeling, but I just wanted to hide from all of them, or leave, or something. As my shivering abated, it hit me. *Why was my DNF so terrible?* I was alive. Given the circumstances, that wasn't guaranteed. Running wasn't my whole life. The more I reflected, the more I realized this wasn't a disaster, or what we call failure, it was a setback. A humbling experience, yes, but not the end of the road. It was the first step in learning to accept failure as part of living intentionally. Telling "the world" (my friends, followers, and family) what happened would be a necessary ingredient to take a step toward mastering the art of living.

When I got back home, I published my DNF blog, and what I found most surprising was how many people were happy that I did not finish, essentially because I lived to tell about it. It was the jolt I needed. It was a hard-earned lesson. For the first time, I felt the distinction between failure as part of the process of growth versus failure as some tragic link to my identity. It became clear to me that when we embrace our failures, we take away their power to shame us. Instead, we can use failure as a catalyst for growth. Ultimately, I'm grateful for that cold, brutal day in the mountains of Tucson. It taught me how to love the edge, accept failure, and come back to tell about it.

Failure is deeply personal. Each of us carries a story, a moment when we fell short, felt defeated, or faced disappointment. These stories aren't just chapters of our lives; they're turning points. When we learn to embrace failure, we rewrite our relationship with discomfort.

We no longer fear the edge; it becomes a frontier of discovery. Failure becomes fuel, and our vocabulary—our inner dialogue—becomes the spark that ignites our potential. The words we whisper to ourselves shape the path forward. When rooted in growth, they cultivate a mindset where we can thrive.

Take a moment to reflect on a recent failure. Maybe it was a project that didn't go as planned, a relationship that ended, or a goal that remained out of reach. What did that experience teach you? Perhaps it revealed an area where you needed growth, resilience, or patience. Perhaps it forced you to reassess your priorities or find a new path forward.

FAILURE IS THE KEY TO GROWTH

As we have explored, failure isn't the end of the road; it's the beginning of the next breakthrough. One of the most remarkable aspects of the human experience is our ability to redefine what is possible by establishing new baselines. Every achievement, no matter how small, becomes a brick in the platform from which we can grow further. What once seemed insurmountable transforms into the foundation for even greater accomplishments.

This isn't just feel-good advice; it's how our brains work. When we perceive something as a failure, our system reacts as if we're under threat. Stress hormones spike, our minds race, and we can easily become stuck replaying what went wrong. However, when we shift our perspective and view failure as feedback, as an opportunity to learn and grow, our brain responds differently. We become more focused, more resilient, and more capable of finding a way forward. That shift in how we interpret the experience changes everything. It doesn't just help us recover; it helps us thrive.

I have sat through countless board of directors' meetings in my business life, and after a particularly contentious board meeting, as I was walking out of the conference room, one of the directors approached me and said that I was too calm during the meeting. I looked at him, puzzled, "too calm?" With all that was happening in there, was that a bad thing? I followed with the quip that he should not confuse calmness with intensity or focus. The emotional outbursts in the meeting were precisely the moment when other directors left their logical business minds behind and started acting with little to no judgment. We certainly did not need more than that. I added that the Navy Seals train a lifetime to be calm in the most harrowing of circumstances; it is how they stay alive. He thanked me for the perspective and wandered to his next meeting.

Those hundreds of board meetings have positively affected my neuroplasticity, the brain's ability to reorganize and strengthen neural pathways. It means that every time I faced a challenge or overcame a setback, I was literally rewiring my brain for resilience and problem-solving. Over time, these pathways strengthened, enabling me to think more critically, tackle greater challenges, and operate at a higher level. I guess you can call it becoming calm.

This process isn't limited to mindset; our bodies mirror this adaptation. At a cellular level, our mitochondria, often referred to as the "powerhouses" of our cells, adapt and grow in response to the demands we place on them. As we increase physical activity, our bodies generate more efficient mitochondria, providing us with greater energy and endurance.[5] This biological adaptation reflects how our mindset and behaviors evolve. With consistent effort, we become stronger and more capable. Consider the process of incremental progress. If you read ten books in a year, the following year, you might aim for twenty. If you run one thousand miles in a year, the next year, you might set your sights on 1,500. Each achievement sets a new standard, not just for what we can do, but for what we believe we are capable of. Over time, these new baselines compound, enabling us to truly perform at the next level. We learn this quickly when we go to the gym. Someone who initially struggles to lift fifty pounds can apply consistent effort and find themselves lifting a hundred pounds within months. The initial "failure" to lift a heavier weight isn't a limitation; it's the start of a process that creates a new baseline of strength. That's how growth happens, not through avoidance, but through progressive adaptation. When we shift our mindset from fearing failure to seeing it as fuel, we wire our brain and body for success. The edge of discomfort isn't the limit; it's the beginning of the next breakthrough. Failure isn't a verdict; it's part of the design for growth. The challenge is learning how to respond to it. That's where reframing comes in.

THE FRAMEWORK FOR TURNING FAILURE INTO FUEL

Reframing failure isn't reserved for extraordinary feats; it's a practice we can apply in everyday life. Here's a simple framework for using failure as a catalyst for growth:

1. Reframe the Narrative

View failure as a teacher, not an adversary. Instead of asking, "Why did this happen to me?" ask, "What can I learn from this?" Recognize that setbacks are not judgments; they are opportunities to adjust and improve. Think of a recent failure and write a brief description of what happened. Then, rewrite the story using empowering language. Highlight what you learned and how it has fueled your growth.

2. Create a Language Shift List

The words we use shape how we process experiences. Write down words or phrases you frequently use that feel limiting and replace them with empowering language. Instead of saying, "I failed," try, "I'm learning." Turn "setback" into "stepping stone." When you shift the language, you shift the meaning.

3. Reflect and Adapt

Take time to reflect on failures. What adjustments can you make next time? Reflection transforms failure into insight and insight into action. Growth is a process of constant refinement.

4. Stretch Your Limits

Set goals that push you just beyond your current baseline. Growth happens when you test the edge of your capacity. Choose one area of your life where you've experienced failure. Set a goal to explore this area with curiosity rather than fear. Write down three actions you can take to approach it with a sense of adventure.

5. Recognize Progress

Progress builds on itself. After reflection, take action. Set a new goal based on what you learned and push slightly beyond your comfort zone. Growth comes not from avoiding failure, but from leaning into it and making adjustments. Celebrate the small wins. Every step forward is proof that you are growing. Even a partial victory is a sign of progress.

Failure isn't the enemy; it's the proving ground. When you shift the story that you tell yourself about failure, you transform it from an obstacle into the raw material for success. Let's remind ourselves that the fuel for our most significant achievements is already within us. All it takes is a shift in perspective, and a willingness to embrace the process of becoming, failures and all. So, take the shot. Apply for the job. Submit the manuscript. Try again. Failure isn't the end; it's the beginning of the next breakthrough.

Failure isn't the enemy; it's the proving ground. When you shift the story that you tell yourself about failure, you transform it from an obstacle into the raw material for success.

CHAPTER 6

GO BIG OR GO HOME

Go Big

We've all heard it—go big or go home. It's catchy, almost irresistible. There's something about it that stirs us, dares us, even taunts us. And maybe that's the point. When we choose to live intentionally, it isn't just a slogan; it's a challenge. A challenge to rise above the ordinary. To step beyond comfort and show up fully for the life we say we want. "Going big" doesn't mean reckless ambition or ego-fueled hustle. It's aligning our actions with our deepest values and dreams and then committing to play full out. When we choose intentionality, we can't stay half in. We can't play small and expect to be fulfilled. Going big is how we honor our potential. It's how we create impact, purpose, and meaning. It reminds us that this life is calling loudly. Because if we're not here to go big, what are we here for?

SETTING BOLD GOALS
THAT CHALLENGE US TO GROW

We all dream. We all imagine more. But somewhere along the way, many of us tend to shrink those dreams down to size. It's not because we lack the talent or potential to do extraordinary things; the path from ordinary to extraordinary is open to every one of us. It might be fear of the unknown, or maybe the pull of security, or the lack of support. We convince ourselves that staying comfortable keeps us safe, that risk is reckless. Often, we talk ourselves out of something before we've even taken the first step. "That's not realistic," we say. Or worse: "That's not me." I used to think that way, too, until I ran six marathons on six continents in six days. That's not a humble brag. It's proof that we're all capable of far more than we realize. During my training, a voice in my head kept saying I was crazy. And that voice got louder every day. But another voice, quieter, steadier, kept asking, "What if?" That's the voice we need to follow.

When we dare to go big, something shifts. The willingness to confront fear and embrace uncertainty becomes a doorway to a life that's not just lived but deeply *felt*. We all have the capacity to stretch our limits, to push beyond what we thought was possible. But potential doesn't activate itself; we must choose to step into the ring. And when we do, when we cross a threshold we once thought was out of reach, the feeling is electric. It's hard to describe, but unmistakable. It changes you. And once you taste that kind of expansion, you won't want to go back. You'll chase it, not for the thrill, but for what it reveals: that you are more capable, more courageous, and more alive than you ever imagined.

THE POWER OF CURIOSITY

Curiosity is the spark that ignites growth. Bold goals often begin with a single question: "What if?" What if I could accomplish something extraordinary? What if I could push past this limit? What if I didn't give up? This seed of curiosity grows as we try new things, learn from experience, and push ourselves further. The more we try, the more curious we become about what lies beyond our current limits. "What will it feel like to accomplish this? What will I learn about myself in the process?" Each attempt fuels the next, creating a cycle of discovery and growth that propels us forward. Consider the Wright brothers. Two bike mechanics from Ohio decided they could build a flying machine. They had no formal engineering training. No government funding. No support from the scientific establishment. Just curiosity and stubborn determination. "What if we could fly?" They didn't have proof, but they had belief. That's the power of curiosity. It drives us to explore, experiment, and push the boundaries of what's possible. We admire people like the Wright brothers from afar. We tell their stories and marvel at what they chose to do. Sadly, though, too many of us do not turn our admiration into action. Twenty-five years ago, I rejected inaction and decided to live my version of bold and courageous living. No permission required. It started with the dream of adventure, and from there, it's become a snowball rolling downhill, picking up mass and momentum. That's the invitation: to create your own version of flight. To act, to build, to believe, right now.

One of the building blocks of living intentionally is pairing our curiosity with action. It is a true foundational element of intentional living. Setting bold goals, stretching beyond what feels comfortable, and embracing each experience with curiosity is how we build a life that is purpose-driven and deeply fulfilling. Every bold goal we set and pursue reinforces our commitment to living with intention, strengthening the framework for all future endeavors.

Think about the boldest goal you've ever set for yourself. Perhaps it was a new job, writing a book, moving to a new location, or launching a business. Was it terrifying at first? If you answered yes, then this is the starting point. Fear is a signal that we are onto something meaningful. Bold goals ignite a fire within us, pulling us toward something greater than our current selves. They demand our focus, our resilience, and our unwavering commitment.

But bold goals aren't just about ambition; they're about growth. When we set the bar high, we're forced to develop new skills, adopt new mindsets, and embrace the unknown. Every step forward, no matter how small, propels us toward a version of ourselves that we might not have otherwise discovered.

HOW TO PUSH PAST SELF-IMPOSED LIMITS

Our limits are rarely real. More often, they're stories we've told ourselves, shaped by past failures, fears, or expectations handed to us by others. To go big, we must unlearn those boundaries and build new ones that reflect our potential, not our past.

It starts with dreaming a little bigger than feels safe. The kind of dream that makes your palms sweat just thinking about it. If a goal doesn't rattle you a bit, it's probably not bold enough to change you. Once that goal is alive in your mind, imagine it. Really imagine it. See it. Feel it. What does success look like? What does it feel like to stand on the other side of it, knowing you made it happen? Visualization isn't just daydreaming; it's brain training. It builds the belief we need when things get hard. Then, act. Don't wait for the perfect time, the perfect plan, or the perfect version of you. Start messy. Take the step, even if it's small or imperfect. Momentum doesn't come from knowing; it comes from doing. And don't do it alone. Bold goals are tough by design. That's why it's so important to surround yourself with people who lift you higher, who challenge your excuses, and who model what's possible. When you're in the right circle, their belief in you amplifies your belief in yourself. Finally, when the inevitable setbacks come, and they *will* come, resist the urge to retreat. Reflect instead. What did you learn? What needs to change? Treat each stumble as data, not defeat. Growth doesn't follow a straight line; it loops and twists and demands that we keep showing up.

WHAT IT FEELS LIKE TO REACH FURTHER

Reaching further is both exhilarating and daunting—a surge of possibility intertwined with the fear of falling short. But it's in that uncertain space where real meaning lives. Every time we step beyond our perceived limits, we affirm something essential: that our goals matter, and that we are worthy of the effort it takes to reach them. Whether it's speaking up in a high-stakes meeting, landing a long-awaited promotion, or finally facing a long-standing fear, each breakthrough strengthens not only our belief in what's possible but also in who we are becoming.

And it doesn't stop with us. Growth is contagious. When we reach, others feel the permission to reach too. I've come to love asking myself my own version of the Wright brothers' question: "What if we could fly?" Only mine sounds more like: *What would it be like to be the CEO of a software company? What if I trained for an Ironman? What would it feel like to speak in front of four thousand people?* Each time I asked, I felt a magnetic pull toward the idea. The energy, the possibility—it became something I wanted to feel in my bones. That's how bold goals begin. A spark of curiosity, then a wave of desire to see how far you can go.

Most recently, I became fascinated by a new challenge: How many pull-ups could I do in twelve hours? I've been doing pull-ups for over two decades. They're a humbling, raw form of strength. Once you can do one, you want to do more. You want to see how fast you can hit one hundred. And if you're wired like me, eventually you wonder: *How many could I do in half a day?* So, I set up shop in my no-frills basement. Just a timer, a chair, some food, music, and that steel bar. I started doing five pull-ups every ninety seconds. Things went smoothly for the first 1,200 reps. Then the "feeling" I had been chasing started to set in. My hands were chafing, my forearms straining. I slowed to five every two minutes. Still, I kept going. At two thousand reps and eleven hours, forty minutes, I stopped, on purpose. Not because I was done, but because I had felt what I came to feel. I had tested my edge. And now I got to wonder again, what's next?

These kinds of challenges don't just change our bodies; they rewire our minds. Each time we go further, we build new beliefs about what we're capable of. We grow our confidence, our resilience, and our capacity to face discomfort head-on. Every win, no matter how small, releases a surge of dopamine, reinforcing our motivation to keep stretching. Over time, we begin to crave that stretch. We stop avoiding adversity and start welcoming it as part of the process. And that matters. Because living a life of meaning isn't about avoiding struggle; it's about embracing it. Fulfillment doesn't come from staying safe. It comes from stepping into something bigger, even when we're not sure how it'll turn out. It comes from going big. And when we do that, we don't just raise the bar for ourselves; we raise it for everyone watching. That's how cultures of courage are built. That's how we create lives worth talking about.

BALANCING AMBITION WITH SELF-AWARENESS

Going big is exhilarating, but it can also be consuming. That inner fire to reach higher, do more, and push past our limits is one of our greatest assets. But left unchecked, that same drive can pull us off course. Ambition, for all its power, is a double-edged sword. It fuels innovation, achievement, and personal transformation. It's what gets us to the starting line and helps carry us to the finish. But if we're not careful, ambition can begin to feed on itself. We start chasing the next goal, the next title, the next milestone, until we forget why we set out in the first place.

I've felt that firsthand. I've answered emails on family vacations, taken calls during moments that should've been sacred, and convinced myself that I was doing it "for us" when really, I had lost sight of what mattered most. I wasn't working toward my *why*; I was caught in the loop of doing more, achieving more, and proving more. The answer isn't to kill ambition; it's to anchor it. To stay aligned with what we truly value. That's where self-awareness comes in. We need to pause and ask: "Why am I pursuing this goal? Is this effort adding value or just feeding the reward loop? What am I sacrificing to chase this?"

For me, it's an ongoing process. I know I tend toward excess, so I build in habits that help me stay centered, such as journaling, breathwork, and quiet time to reflect. These moments don't slow me down; they recalibrate me. They help me live intentionally, not reactively.

I've also learned to let go of old benchmarks. I don't run as fast as I used to, but that's not failure. That's wisdom. That's growth with grace. Ambition should lift us, not drain us. It should be a source of purpose, not pressure. And when we get that balance right, we discover the deeper reward, not the title, not the money, but the peace of knowing we lived aligned with who we are and what really matters.

YEARLY GOALS AND LONG-TERM DEVELOPMENT

Big goals take time. The most meaningful progress doesn't come from overnight wins; it comes from steady, intentional effort over the long haul. That's why yearly goals are so powerful. They become markers along the way, anchoring our bold vision to something actionable. But here's the key: don't just set goals for the sake of productivity. Set them with purpose. Start by stepping back and asking: "What's the big picture? Where do I want to be in three, five, even ten years? What kind of life am I building?" Once that vision is clear, pick three to five goals for this year that move you closer. Make them bold but grounded. Break each one down into real, tangible steps. And as the year unfolds, check in often. Not to micromanage, but to stay aligned. Adjust when necessary. Not to make it easier, but to keep it meaningful.

And don't forget to celebrate the progress. Every small win builds confidence. Every milestone is a moment to pause and appreciate how far you've come. This is the compounding power of consistent effort; it strengthens our belief that growth is not just possible but inevitable when we stay the course. Trust the process. Be patient. The tree doesn't grow overnight. Give it time, and its roots will anchor something unshakable.

FINDING A COMMUNITY OF BIG DREAMERS

We are not meant to go big alone. Every ambitious journey is easier when we're surrounded by people who get it, who believe in dreaming beyond what's typical, and who won't settle for playing small. It is important to find people who reflect your mindset, even if their dreams are different. Some are training for an Ironman race. Others are launching nonprofits or writing books. Their energy, their hunger, and their belief is contagious. Use it. Social media can be a surprising source of inspiration. You'll find creators, athletes, podcasters, and thinkers—people testing their edge and showing what's possible. Learn from them. Study what worked for them. Let their courage ignite your own.

Once you've named your bold goals, invite others in. Share your vision. Ask for feedback. Collaborate. Whether you're training for a marathon or starting a company, a community can keep you moving when you'd otherwise stall. Even more than strategy, community provides "emotional fuel." It keeps you accountable when motivation wanes. It reminds you that you're not crazy for wanting more. A strong circle lifts you up, dares you to reach further, and shows you what's possible on the other side of discomfort. A few years ago, I found my people in a group of forty-something triathletes. We trained, pushed, and celebrated together. We failed together. But most importantly, we believed in each other. And belief, shared belief, is rocket fuel.

> A strong circle lifts you up, dares you
> to reach further, and shows you what's
> possible on the other side of discomfort.

Over time, I've come to see that "go big or go home" isn't just a slogan; it's a way of life. It's an invitation to live fully, to move through fear, and to choose growth, even when it's hard. Especially when it's hard, because this path will test you; it will stretch you, shake you, and make you question everything. But in meeting each challenge, you grow stronger. You connect with who you are and begin to glimpse who you're meant to become. So set bold goals. Chase wild ideas. Ask the questions that scare you. Let your curiosity lead. And find joy not just in reaching the summit, but in how the climb changes you. Because that's the real reward. Not the medal. Not the title. But the transformation.

THE PURSUIT OF MASTERY: HOW TO BECOME THE BEST AT WHAT YOU DO

A few years ago, someone asked me what my superpower was. At first, I dismissed it as one of those throwaway questions, but then I gave it real thought. It wasn't intelligence, talent, or luck; it was something more profound. The path to mastery isn't complicated. It just requires three things: the C^3 powerhouse.

- **Courage** to start

- **Commitment** to continue

- **Consistency** to master

Mastery isn't about raw talent or luck. It's about showing up, repeatedly, in pursuit of something greater. The world's top performers, whether athletes, artists, entrepreneurs, or leaders, don't succeed because they are gifted. They succeed because they have mastered the discipline of C³, and it is something that I share with them.

> Mastery isn't about raw talent or luck.
> It's about showing up, repeatedly, in
> pursuit of something greater.

WHY C³ IS A SUPERPOWER

Courage: It's the entry point. Without courage, commitment and consistency don't happen. Many people hesitate at the doorstep of change, fearing failure, discomfort, or the unknown. True courage isn't the absence of fear; it's the decision to act despite it. Courage is what gets us started.

Commitment: This is where most people falter. Commitment means making a deliberate choice, setting intentions, and following through even when motivation fades. It is an explicit agreement with ourselves for how seriously we take our goals. It's the glue between courage and consistency, the promise that keeps us moving forward when things get hard. Ultimately, we cannot let ourselves down.

Consistency: The most powerful of the three because it compounds over time. Mastery isn't built through occasional big efforts, but through small, deliberate actions repeated day after day. The greatest performers don't see repetition as imprisoning or boring; they embrace it as the gateway to excellence and freedom. When we shift from seeing consistency as a chore to a privilege, everything changes.

THE BIOLOGY BEHIND C³:

Neuroscience of Habits: The brain strengthens neural pathways through repeated actions. The more we do something, the easier it becomes, which is why repetition is essential to mastery.

Dopamine and Motivation: Consistency fuels dopamine, but not just from achieving big wins. Dopamine is also released when we gain momentum through small, repeated actions. This is what keeps us engaged and progressing.

The Homeostasis Challenge: Our bodies and minds crave equilibrium, but growth requires disruption. Every time we push ourselves beyond what's comfortable, we trigger adaptation. Mastery is built through this continuous process of challenge, adaptation, and repetition.

EMBRACE THE C³ FRAMEWORK FOR INTENTIONAL LIVING

Mastery isn't a one-time decision; it's a lifelong process of courage, commitment, and consistency. Here's how to apply it:

- **Assess Your Courage Level:** We all have courage within us. The key is identifying the fears or excuses preventing action and moving forward anyway.

- **Make a Bold Commitment:** Define a clear, measurable commitment that challenges your limits. Then, say your commitment out loud in the mirror—again and again—until you feel it in your bones.

- **Build Systems for Consistency:** It's not about willpower; it's about creating an environment that supports the habit.

The best in the world don't just practice; they fall in love with the process. Consistency is the pure representation of the signal through the noise of life. It allows us to become and to find joy in the repetition because the results it creates are remarkable.

THE PATH TO THE TOP 1 PERCENT: MASTERY THROUGH INTENTIONALITY

What does it take to become world-class at something? Most people assume that elite performance is reserved for those with extraordinary talent or an unfair advantage; that the top 1 percent are born gifted. But that's a myth. What we learn is that the top 1 percent aren't necessarily the most talented; they're the most intentional. They apply specific principles over decades, compounding small advantages into massive success. Talent matters less than consistency and purpose.

Let me give you an example. For 4,500+ days in a row, I have published a blog post. Some days it was a page, other days just a paragraph, but I never missed a day. Over time, that consistency compounded into something remarkable. I became a more skillful writer. I could feel it; there was less effort, the color of my words came through, and I was energized by my new skill. But here's the thing: it wasn't talent that got me there. It was intentionality. The act of showing up every day and writing consistently refined my craft. The same pattern has repeated itself in other areas of my life: running marathons, building businesses, and personal growth. Time and again, intentionality won over talent.

For what it's worth, this isn't the only area where I've pushed myself into the top 1 percent. Leveraging C^3 plus a set of clear intentions,

I approach each pursuit with purpose and commit fully to the process and time required. The result? Almost inevitably, I find myself among the top performers. This isn't luck; it's a formula. And I believe it's not just possible, but probable that anyone can achieve the same, provided they choose to live with intention.

1. Play the Long Game

Most people quit too soon. The difference between those who achieve mastery and those who plateau is often persistence. We cannot let ourselves become bored over time. When I was training for Ironman, I created a formula for my days, and it looked very similar every day. Get up at 4:20 a.m., get on the bike, ride fifty miles, eat a high-protein breakfast, go to work, eat two peanut butter and jelly sandwiches, after work go to the pool or for a run, eat a big dinner, and get to bed around 11:00 p.m. I did this just about every day for five years. I loved every day. I was excited to eat those PB&Js every day. I wanted to get back on the bike, and on and on. Every day, we can love what we do. The more I loved it, the longer I was able to stick with the plan. If we want to be in the top 1 percent, then we must think in years, not days, stick with the plan, and feel good about it as we move along.

- Warren Buffett built his fortune not just through smart investing but through time in the market; his greatest asset was longevity.

- Tom Brady wasn't the most talented quarterback early in his career, but his obsession with improvement over twenty-plus years made him the greatest of all time.

- Long marriages aren't the result of avoiding problems, but of choosing to work through them year after year, when others give up. I have now been married for thirty-seven-plus years, and I can attest to the fact that we have both committed to the long game and have every intention of being together for our lifetime.

To rise to the top, commit to the long haul. Outlast yourself, and then the competition.

2. Develop an Obsession with Improvement

The one-percenters are never satisfied with "good enough." They constantly seek better strategies, refine their skills, and push beyond their current limits.

- **Continuous Improvement:** Small, daily refinements create unstoppable momentum. This should make it easier, not harder. We don't even need big pushes; we just need to bring our C^3 to the task, and the rest comes along.

- **Deliberate Practice:** Focus not just on repetition, but on looking for weak points, and find joy in knowing that you are figuring it out. A real feedback loop and the ability to work on the details are the true catalysts for improvement.

- **Seek Discomfort:** Sadly, comfort is the enemy of growth. Over time, we learn that growth only happens when we push beyond our current capacity. Finding the limits and the edges is an accomplishment that we should be proud of and look for every day.

Ultimately, if we want to be in the top 1 percent, we must do more than improve our skills; we must evolve our identity. That means accepting the full implications of the path: the sacrifice, the discipline, the solitude, and the commitment it demands. But once you embrace that this life comes with trade-offs and welcome them, you stop resisting and start rising. That's when everything aligns. That's when the real growth begins.

3. Create Unfair Advantages

I found out that the highest achievers don't just work harder, they also work *smarter*. They position themselves where they have a distinct edge. It's like the best coach that you have ever met in your life, when they tell you those "secrets" to making it work. My brother-in-law, Richard, was a prime example of this. He was a scratch golfer, and every time we went to play golf, he talked about shots in a very different way than I thought about them. He strategized every shot, and it saved him stroke after stroke. It propelled him to win his club championship against a lot of great golfers, all because he created his version of an unfair advantage.

- **Find Leverage:** Invest in skills that multiply your efforts, like communication, networking, and leadership.

- **Own Unique Knowledge:** The best in any field develops specialized expertise that few others have.

- **Use Systems and Automation:** Don't rely on willpower; instead, build routines and habits that make elite performance automatic.

The top 1 percent don't play by the same rules as everyone else; they create their own.

4. Build a Resilient Mindset

Failure is inevitable. The difference between the top 1 percent and everyone else is their ability to *keep going*.

- **Embrace Rejection:** Every "no" gets you closer to "yes."

- **Reframe Setbacks:** Failure is feedback. It's data. Use it.

- **Master Emotional Discipline:** Emotional resilience, which is your ability to stay calm, focused, and disciplined under stress, is often the key to long-term success.

Your ability to stay in the game when things get tough is one of the most powerful predictors of success.

5. Surround Yourself with Excellence

Success isn't a solo endeavor. The people you surround yourself with influence your trajectory.

- **Find Mentors:** who have already achieved what you want.

- **Create a High-Performance Peer Group:** that challenges and supports you.

- **Eliminate Toxic Influences:** such as energy-draining people and negative environments that will slow your ascent.

Want to be in the top 1 percent? Surround yourself with people who are already there. OK, so you might say that you don't have access to people who are in the top 1 percent, so here is the life hack I recommend: YouTube, TED Talks, and podcasts. You can find some of the best in the world sharing their stories, their insights, and their experiences, for free, on these platforms and other social media platforms. You can learn from the best in our modern content-rich world.

When I was working to become a better public speaker and to see how the smartest people in the world thought, I endeavored to use the TED Talk platform as my knowledge base and insight engine. So, in one year, I watched one thousand TED talks. I did most of that while running on a treadmill, doing a different version of James Clear's habit stacking[1]; mine was activity stacking. But wow, what a result I got. I "hung out" with A LOT of very smart people, learned a ton, got my running in, and put myself on the path to peak performance. There is always a way; we just need to set the right intention, and we can get there.

6. Master the Art of Consistency

At the top, talent matters far less than consistency. What separates the elite from the average is not missing days.

- The best athletes don't train when they feel like it—they train *according to the plan.*

- The best investors don't chase trends—they follow *consistent principles.*

- The best relationships don't last because of luck—they last because of *consistent effort.*

Excellence isn't about massive efforts in short bursts; it's about small, disciplined actions repeated daily over years.

THE 1 PERCENT MINDSET

Getting to the top 1 percent is not about chasing overnight success. It's about:

- **Time in the Game:** Most people give up too early.

- **Continuous Improvement:** Small, daily progress compounds.

- **Creating Unfair Advantages:** Work smarter, not only harder.

- **Building Resilience:** The best don't avoid failure; they embrace it.

- **Surrounding Yourself with Excellence:** The right people will accelerate your growth.

- **Relentless Consistency:** Small wins daily build massive results over time

Mastery isn't about luck; it's about choice. The top 1 percent follow a process. They clarify what they want, they show up consistently, and they let the power of compounding work its magic over time. And here's the best part: this formula works for anyone. You don't need to be gifted; you just need to be intentional. The path to the top 1 percent isn't easy, but it's simple. The question is: Are you willing to show up every day and do the work?

CHAPTER 7

FINDING MEANING THROUGH SUFFERING

The Call Beneath the Comfort

We live in a world that whispers constantly: Seek ease. Avoid discomfort. Find what feels good and hold on tight. But beneath the surface, something deeper calls us. Comfort may feel safe, but it rarely transforms us. Real growth lives in the struggle, in the friction between who we are and who we're meant to become. Much of what we call suffering doesn't arise from pain itself but from attachment. Attachment to outcomes, expectations, identities, and illusions of control. We suffer not because of what is but because of what we think should be. We want something so badly that we convince ourselves we need it to be whole. And when reality doesn't match the script we've written, we feel lost. But suffering can be a mirror. It reveals what we cling to, what we fear, and what we believe defines us. And in doing so, it gives us a choice: resist or embrace it. When we stop running and start

115

listening, suffering becomes a sacred invitation. A path not to despair but to awakening. To embrace suffering is not to seek it but to accept it when it arrives, to honor it as part of the human experience. In that space, we begin to understand ourselves more fully. We strip away the noise, the false needs, the ego's grip. And what remains is something real: clarity, presence, peace. Because when we stop demanding that life always feels good, we start discovering what it means to feel whole.

THE TAHOE 200: WHEN SUFFERING BROKE ME OPEN

I was at mile 180 of the Tahoe 200, trying to convince myself that "only twenty miles to go" meant something. It didn't. My ankle was twice its normal size, throbbing with every step. Pain had settled in like a second heartbeat. Those twenty miles might as well have been a thousand. Without my trekking poles, I'd have been crawling through the dirt. Seventy-six hours in, the world was a blur of trail dust, hallucinations, and anguish. On a typical day, I could knock out twenty miles before lunch. But now? I was staring down another eighteen hours of grinding. The math was cruel. And yet, quitting wasn't on the table. It never had been. But the voices in my head wouldn't stop: *Why a two-hundred-mile race? What are you still trying to prove? Hadn't ten marathons this year, or six marathons on six continents in six days, been enough?*

Somewhere along the way, I had fused my identity with the extremes. Pushing myself became the currency I used to justify my existence. Capability had quietly become an obligation. Suffering had become the toll I was willing to pay to feel worthy. As I left the aid station and looked up at yet another mountain climb, I couldn't help but laugh at my own audacity. *Great idea, genius. You really nailed it this time.* So, I leaned in. One foot, then the other. Two miles per hour when I was lucky. Often slower. The miles dragged by like centuries. And then mile 205. Not 200, of course. The universe doesn't round down. One last descent, I came around the final bend, I saw the finish line, and I broke. Tears poured down my face. My ankle was still screaming, but that wasn't it. Certainly not joy. It was something deeper, something I hadn't expected.

I was undone.

For twenty years, I had been running toward goals, away from doubts, around the edges of myself. And there, at the edge of physical collapse, I finally arrived at my truth:

I was enough.

Not because I finished.

Not because I conquered the race.

But because I stopped needing to prove it.

I began to understand what suffering had been trying to teach me all along. Suffering isn't just pain; it's attachment. It clings to the idea that we're only as valuable as what we accomplish, that we must earn our place, and that we are only worthy when we win. But in those final steps, I let it go. The striving, the proving, the armor, it all cracked open. And what poured through was self-love. Unconditional. Unpolished. Real.

Was this Maslow's self-actualization? Was this what the monks meant by freedom from attachment? Maybe. All I know is that I had crossed some invisible threshold. And on the other side wasn't a medal or a headline or a crowd. It was stillness. Clarity. A kind of quiet reverence for simply being alive. I had found my way to a place where peak performance and complete acceptance of my human condition weren't at odds; they were two sides of the same coin. I had found what it means to live with intention, not just to push limits but to embrace what lay beyond and find something that striving couldn't teach. Living intentionally isn't just about going big. It's about going deep. It's about meeting yourself in the dark and not turning away, or as S. N. Behrman suggested, "at the end of every road you meet yourself." Amazing doesn't begin to cover it.

THE JOURNEY BEYOND DISCOMFORT

We talk a lot about discomfort as a pathway to growth, how pushing through physical, mental, and emotional barriers expands our capacity and strengthens our resolve. Discomfort is temporary. It's a test of resilience and mental strength. Remember, it never rises to the level of quit. But suffering is different; it goes deeper and it is existential. It strips us down to the core, when the only thing left to carry us forward is our mind and our soul, forcing us to confront the fundamental questions: "Why am I doing this? Who am I beyond this pain? What happens if I can't keep going?"

The line between discomfort and suffering is the moment when life stops being about accomplishment and becomes a confrontation with the self. During those endless miles in Tahoe, I learned that suffering isn't just about physical pain. It's about facing the void between who we think we should be and who we are. It's about the stories we tell ourselves and the masks we wear. When suffering breaks us open, these stories shatter, leaving us naked before ourselves. At the end of the road, we meet ourselves.

BEING MINDFUL OF SUFFERING

Buddhism teaches that suffering—*dukkha*—is not just inevitable; it's essential for awakening. The First Noble Truth isn't a condemnation of life, but an invitation to see it clearly. We don't suffer because life is cruel; we suffer because we resist what is. Our attachments—to outcomes, to identity, to control—create the very suffering we try to escape. When we demand that life unfold a certain way, and it doesn't, we find ourselves in turmoil.

Nowhere is this more evident than in the era of social media. Platforms like Instagram and TikTok have turned comparison into a reflex. We scroll through highly curated versions of other people's lives—the wins, the perfect bodies, the luxurious vacations—and absorb the illusion that we're falling behind. We become attached to outcomes that aren't even real. Social media distorts reality. It presents life as a relentless highlight reel, where struggle and discomfort are filtered out and buried beneath smiles and filters. But life isn't meant to be a seamless stream of wins and dopamine hits. As Buddhism reminds us, suffering stems from attachment, and in the digital age, we are constantly bombarded with illusions that amplify that attachment. We expect life to match the glossy perfection we see on our screens. And when it doesn't, we feel like we've failed. This constant comparison drives a sense of inadequacy. It makes us forget that discomfort isn't failure, it's the raw material of growth. We scroll to escape the discomfort of real life, numbing ourselves instead of facing that which would set us free. We know that we can't just "quit" social media and expect clarity to appear. If we want to live more mindfully, we must replace it with something better.

I've found my alternative by living more fully. When I run a hundred-mile race, prepare for a board meeting, write my blog, or coach a client, I'm not checking social media. I'm not thinking about likes or curated images. I'm in it. I'm present. I see more clearly. I'm aligned with my *why*. These are the moments that ground me, where I feel productive, connected, and fulfilled. Not because they're easy, but because they're real. This is what living intentionally looks like. It's not about escaping discomfort. It's about choosing presence over distraction, purpose over performance, and life over illusion.

Kylie Kelce, in her podcast *Not Gonna Lie*, openly discusses the emotional toll of social media criticism and the constant pressure to meet unrealistic expectations. Reflecting on the negativity she's encountered online, she says, "I can't get over the fact that you actually typed this into Twitter," capturing the hurt that comes with public scrutiny.[1] Kelce's experience highlights how social media distorts reality, making us more attached to external validation and vulnerable to suffering when that validation isn't received. As was highlighted earlier, Buddhism teaches that attachment to identity and outcomes creates suffering, and social media fuels both. When we post a picture, we often tie our sense of worth to the number of likes and comments. When those numbers fall short, we suffer. Not because life itself is cruel, but because we've tied our self-worth to an expectation that is inextricably linked to fleeting digital metrics.

As Kelce's experience suggests, the first step is awareness, seeing the illusion for what it is and choosing to ground ourselves in reality, rather than the digital mirage. True strength comes not from appearing flawless but from finding peace within the chaos of imperfection. We may not all fully embrace the depth of the Buddhist Four Noble Truths, but with the right effort, mindfulness, and focus, suffering can become a teacher rather than an enemy. When we stop resisting discomfort, it stops being a threat and becomes a doorway, an entry point to deeper growth and understanding.

THE STOIC VIEW OF SUFFERING

Ryan Holiday's *The Obstacle Is the Way* echoes this same idea through the lens of Stoicism. The Stoics believe that suffering and adversity are not to be feared; they are opportunities to practice virtue. Courage, resilience, patience, and wisdom are forged through suffering. Holiday's core message is simple but profound: the obstacle becomes the way. When we face suffering, we have a choice. We can see it as an unfair setback or as a training ground. We can resist it, or we can use it to sharpen ourselves.[2] Marcus Aurelius wrote: "What stands in the way becomes the way."[3] In other words, the thing that challenges us isn't blocking the path; it *is* the path. Holiday argues that suffering is a chance to practice emotional control. When we respond thoughtfully rather than reactively, we develop the mental strength to thrive in any circumstance. The suffering isn't the problem. How we respond to it is.[4]

THE DANGER OF COMFORT

What suffering can do for us, as I learned at Tahoe, is that it can bring us to a deeper sense of self-actualization, which is rarely found through comfort. Suffering strips away pretense. It reveals what lies beneath the surface. But if we are to go below the surface, we are going to need to address how we are evolving and living. Think of this: in 2024, Netflix reported that its subscribers spent an average of almost two hours daily on the platform, amounting to over

180 billion hours of viewing across the year.[5] This staggering figure underscores a broader societal trend: the extensive consumption of digital media as a means to fill time, seek entertainment, or escape from daily stress.

While engaging with media can offer relaxation and enjoyment, excessive consumption often serves as a distraction from personal growth and self-reflection. Binge-watching in particular has been linked to negative outcomes such as poor sleep quality, insomnia, and fatigue.[6] By immersing ourselves in continuous streams of content, we may inadvertently avoid confronting challenges or discomforts that are essential for personal development. If we, however, can get ourselves to face our discomforts directly, we transform them into opportunities for growth. Alternatively, when we use media consumption to sidestep these uncomfortable emotions, we miss the chance to engage deeply with our inner selves.

To live intentionally means to be mindful of how we allocate our time and attention. Recognizing the allure and the danger of endless content, we can choose to set boundaries on media consumption, creating space for activities that foster self-awareness, learning, and genuine connection. By doing so, we confront the discomforts we've been avoiding, paving the way toward self-actualization and a more fulfilling life.

THE ALCHEMY OF TRANSFORMATION

What I discovered in those mountain miles was that suffering has a strange alchemy. When we stop resisting it, when we lean into the pain with curiosity instead of fear, something shifts. The suffering doesn't disappear, but it transforms. It becomes a crucible for growth, a doorway to understanding. I watched an interview on YouTube with Kat Edwards Anderson, a professional ultra-runner, after completing the 2024 Moab 240—one of the toughest ultramarathons in the world. I have always been curious about this race, so I innocently listened to her recap the race, and then she floored me when she reflected on the shift that happens when you stop chasing limits and start discovering how good you can be: "The further I get outside my comfort zone, the more mistakes I make, the more failures I have. They all raise the bar up a little bit. They all make you better as you continue to grow. Your capacity for your limit rises with you. So, I think now, instead of chasing the proverbial limit, my goal moreso is to figure out how good I can be. How good I can be as an athlete, as a human, as a family member, as a friend. Those things, I think, mean so much more than a physical athletic limit."[7]

This is what Viktor E. Frankl, author of *Man's Search for Meaning*, meant when he wrote about finding meaning in suffering. It's not about seeking suffering for its own sake. It's about recognizing that our deepest growth often comes through our greatest challenges, discovering the full scope of our personal potential.[8] It's not just about running farther or working harder; it's about becoming more. It's about expanding our capacity, not just as an athlete or a professional, but as a human being. When faced with moments of doubt, fear, or suffering, we can ask ourselves: "What would happen if I found a way?" What we learn from these extreme examples is the simple lesson that when we accept suffering, we start to grow. We build resilience, develop new skills, and learn to trust ourselves. True growth isn't about finding the limit; it's about discovering how far we can go when we embrace suffering in every part of life. When we're stripped of everything else, we discover what truly matters.

HOW TO FIND MEANING THROUGH SUFFERING

1. Reframe the Experience

Instead of viewing suffering as punishment, see it as a path to discovery. Ask yourself: "What is this teaching me? What strength can I develop through this?"

2. Lean Into the Process

Frankl's insight was that meaning is found *through* suffering, not despite it. Stop trying to avoid pain; embrace it as a necessary step toward self-discovery.

3. Find Community

Shared suffering creates deep bonds. Don't isolate yourself in your pain.

4. Maintain Perspective

Remember that suffering is temporary, even when it feels eternal.

5. Let Go of the Outcome

Suffering becomes unbearable when we tie it to a specific outcome. Let go of needing a certain result. Growth and appreciating the process are the goals.

6. Find a Higher Purpose

Suffering becomes meaningful when it connects to something bigger than you. Why are you pushing through this? What's the larger story? What is this experience teaching you about yourself, about life?

BEYOND THE FINISH LINE

Back at Tahoe, crossing that finish line wasn't really about the medal or the achievement. It was about discovering that I could face my deepest fears and keep going. That I could be broken open and find something beautiful inside. That suffering wasn't my enemy; it was my teacher. We can't avoid suffering, but we can choose how we meet it. We can let it break us, or we can let it break us open. We can resist it, or we can let it teach us. We can see it as punishment, or we can recognize it as transformation. The choice is always ours. And sometimes, in those darkest miles when everything hurts and we're not sure we can take another step, we discover that suffering isn't just something to endure; it's the very thing that sets us free because suffering isn't the enemy. It's the doorway. And what lies beyond that doorway is nothing less than our true selves, waiting to be discovered.

> We can't avoid suffering, but we can choose how we meet it. We can let it break us, or we can let it break us open. We can resist it, or we can let it teach us. We can see it as punishment, or we can recognize it as transformation. The choice is always ours.

CHAPTER 8

THE POWER OF CONNECTION

The Path We Are On

Life has a way of teaching us simple, profound truths, and one of them is this: the more we give to our community, the stronger we all become. Whether it's a neighborhood, a network of colleagues, or even a digital space where people gather around a shared purpose, our communities are more than just groups; we are reflections of one another. Connecting isn't just about acts of service. It's about truly seeing the people around us, recognizing their struggles, celebrating their victories, and standing beside them through it all. The strength of our connections is built in these moments, not through grand gestures, but through the simple willingness to show up, listen, and be present. In today's fast-paced, hyper-individualistic world, it's easy to focus only on our personal goals and ambitions. But when we shift our attention outward, when we invest in others, support their dreams, and lift them in their struggles, we create a ripple effect that extends far beyond what we can see. We don't just help others grow; we grow too. Connection isn't an obligation; it's an opportunity. An opportunity to live intentionally, to forge deeper bonds, and to remind ourselves that life's most meaningful moments are found in our shared communities.

WHAT CONNECTION IS ALL ABOUT

Have you ever texted someone…while they were standing right next to you? We've all done it. In a world wired for communication, genuine connection is becoming harder to find. Despite the constant notifications, video calls, and online communities, people are lonelier than ever. It's not because we don't care. It's because disconnection is easy and connection takes effort. There isn't someone to blame for our doom-scrolling on TikTok or binge-watching a Netflix series; it's just easier to stay on the couch than go outside and hang out. Think about it: you can Instacart your groceries, work remotely, send a quick text rather than have a conversation, or lose yourself in a television series rather than engage with the world around you. Soon, you'll be able to ride in a driverless taxi and never make eye contact with another person.

It's not that any of these things are inherently bad. But together, they chip away at something essential, our human need to belong. It didn't happen all at once. We're like the frog in the pot, not noticing the water getting warmer and warmer. One day, we wake up and realize we feel isolated, disengaged, and unsure how to reach out again. But here's the good news: we're wired to connect. Deeply. Meaningfully. Authentically.

We are naturally made to connect, but it isn't just about proximity or communication; it's about resonance. It's about the emotional, mental, and sometimes even spiritual bond we form with others and how those bonds shape who we are. We're wired for real connection; it's literally in our DNA. That flutter in our chest when someone truly gets us, that warmth when we share a genuine laugh, the comfort of a friend's presence during tough times: no amount of perfectly filtered Instagram posts can replace these moments. Living intentionally is our way back to a connected state. It is not too late to reconnect, and in fact, it is vital for our future.

Connection is powerful because it reminds us that we are not alone. It reaffirms our place in the world and our sense of belonging. When we connect with someone on a meaningful level, we share a piece of ourselves, our stories, our fears, and our dreams. In return, we receive validation, empathy, and support. There's comfort in hearing that someone else struggles like we do, that they are also working through challenges, from relationships to jobs to finances and everything in between. The idea of mutual issues (a.k.a. empathy) has the power to uplift us in moments of despair, challenge us to grow, and inspire us to keep moving forward when life feels hard.

The connections we make can become the lifeblood of our personal journey. They shape our identities, influence our decisions, and help us see possibilities we might never have considered on our own. We learn from each other, copy each other, and support each other. It's what makes us different from all other species that inhabit the earth. More than anything, connection is what makes us human. It's why we are all still here, eight billion or so of us. Being human drives us to care for one another, to create, to love, and to contribute to something bigger than ourselves. But here's the thing, connection doesn't happen by accident. It requires intention. We must seek it out, nurture it, and show up for it even when it's uncomfortable or inconvenient.

And nowhere is this clearer than in the business world, where connection can be reduced to pixels on a screen. All too often, it would be easy to have a Zoom call and sit in our comfortable office, coffee in hand, just staring at a screen and thinking this is a relationship. What I have figured out over the years is that whenever I get on an airplane or in the car to go visit a customer or see their facility, something different happens. The customer talks to me differently, they tell me more, and they show me how their business operates. I also see and experience it differently. Even if it's just in their office, I can get a sense of what matters to them and how I can better relate.

Not only does it create a stronger connection between us, but it also makes me more memorable. They know that I took the time to come visit, to make them more important, and to show them how deeply I am interested in their business and their challenges. Every time I leave one of my visits, I reflect on how powerful the experience was and the positive impact that it made for all. There is no world where Zoom can replace what I am able to experience in person. Life is not about convenience; it's about presence. It's about showing up. Because in the end, it's not the slides we share or the products we pitch that people remember; it's how we made them feel. And that kind of resonance only happens when we're fully present.

The power of connection is in its ability to transform not only our lives, but also the lives of those we touch. It is through connection that we find purpose, meaning, and fulfillment. What I've learned is we cannot wait for an invitation, or for the phone to ring, or for an email to get connected. We need to take the lead. If we want to do something with someone, then we need to ask. It's as simple as sending a text inviting someone for coffee, or a hike, or to go to a new exhibit at the local museum.

In the end, the path back to each other isn't complicated. It just requires something increasingly rare in our world of instant gratification: intention. The willingness to be a little uncomfortable, a little vulnerable, a little more present. When all is said and done, no one ever looks back on their life and wishes they'd spent more time scrolling.

THE COLLECTIVE: SURROUNDING OURSELVES WITH SUPPORTIVE PEOPLE

We are, by nature, social creatures, wired for connection. I've seen it in every part of my life, from leadership teams to endurance races to late-night conversations with friends. When we feel seen, supported, and challenged by others, something inside us lights up. It's not just emotional; it's deeply human. I may not be a neuroscientist, but I've come to understand that our brains are tuned to respond to belonging. That's why the people we surround ourselves with matter more than we realize. I call this inner circle our "collective"—the small, intentional group of people who are closest to us and have the most significant influence on how we think, act, and grow. These aren't just casual acquaintances; they're our mirrors, our motivators, and our grounding force. Their energy influences ours, their mindset affects how we think, and their behavior subtly molds our own. Over time, without even realizing it, we either rise or drift depending on who's around us. The adage from Jim Rohn that you are the average of the five people you spend the most time with rings more true the older I get. But it's not just about surrounding ourselves with cheerleaders. A strong collective also stretches us, introducing new perspectives, asking hard questions, and holding us accountable to the version of ourselves we're striving to become. Genuine connection happens not when everyone agrees but when we open ourselves to differing perspectives and are willing to learn from those who challenge us to think beyond our current frame. In a strong collective, there is space for both comfort and friction. That's where the real growth happens. We find support during moments of doubt and celebration in moments of triumph. Our group becomes our safety net, our source of accountability, and our cheerleading squad all at once.

Connection isn't just a nice-to-have—it's hardwired into our biology. Human connection triggers the release of oxytocin, the "bonding hormone," which lowers stress and increases feelings of trust and psychological safety. Chronic loneliness, by contrast, activates the body's stress response and raises cortisol levels, ultimately weakening the immune system and fueling inflammation. This isn't just about happiness. It's about health, vitality, and resilience. A seventy-five-year longitudinal study from Harvard concluded that the single most important predictor of long-term well-being isn't wealth or success, it's the quality of our relationships.[1] The right community holds you. It's a place where you can feel safe enough and brave enough to say how you feel and not be afraid to try again. We can be worthy and a work in progress. This is the essence of the collective: not just support but belief. Not just challenge, but care. It's the kind of space that expands toward who you want to become and honors who you are now.

This is the essence of the collective: not just
support but belief. Not just challenge, but care. It's
the kind of space that expands toward who you
want to become and honors who you are now.

WHO ARE THE FIVE PEOPLE?

Think about the idea of your inner circle. Who are the five people you engage with most frequently? These could be colleagues, friends, family members, mentors, or even online communities. Do they inspire, challenge, and support your goals? Or do they drain your energy, create self-doubt, and pull you away from your aspirations?

Let's refine what these five people might represent:

- **The Mentor:** Someone with more experience who offers guidance, wisdom, and feedback.

- **The Peer Challenger:** A friend or colleague who pushes you to think differently, take risks, and step outside your comfort zone.

- **The Emotional Anchor:** Someone who provides stability and helps you stay grounded during turbulent times.

- **The Cheerleader:** A supportive individual who celebrates your wins and encourages you when you feel like giving up.

- **The Learner:** Someone who is growing alongside you, exchanging insights and experiences as you both push toward new goals.

Who comes to mind as you reflect on each of these roles in your life? It's a powerful exercise to regularly revisit an intentional inventory of who is shaping your mindset and your momentum. These roles are not rigid; they evolve as we do. Life shifts, priorities change, and so do the people who occupy our inner circle. But what remains constant is our responsibility to choose wisely. We must curate our circle with intention, surrounding ourselves with those who lift us, not limit us. The energy, belief systems, and habits of those closest to us don't just influence how we think; they construct the very architecture of our reality.

BUILDING A COLLECTIVE WITH INTENTION

Building a collective takes time and effort. It requires intentionality in the relationships we cultivate and the communities we join. But once we do the work to establish it, we'll unlock a powerful source of energy, inspiration, and resilience that can propel us toward living our best lives.

- **Audit Your Inner Circle:** Take stock of the five people you spend the most time with. Are they aligned with your values and goals?

- **Seek Diversity of Thought:** Don't just surround yourself with people who agree with you. Growth comes from friction and challenge.

- **Create Space for Vulnerability:** True connection happens when you feel safe enough to be seen as you are.

- **Give as Much as You Receive:** Connection is a two-way street. Be the kind of person you want to attract.

When we surround ourselves with people who challenge us, inspire us, and stand by us, we create a world that fuels our growth. And as we grow, we lift others with us. Connection isn't just a source of strength; it's a catalyst for becoming the best version of ourselves.

HOW CONNECTION HAS EVOLVED OVER HUMAN HISTORY

Connection is not a new concept. It has been at the heart of human existence since the dawn of time. Our ability to connect and collaborate is one of the primary reasons Homo sapiens became the dominant species on the planet. In early human history, connection was a matter of survival. Tribes formed to share resources, protect one another, and ensure the continuity of their communities. For centuries, connection wasn't just a luxury; it was a necessity. Over time, these connections evolved into more complex social structures—families, communities, nations—each with its own rules and cultural norms. We moved from farming to an industrial world, to a computing world, to a social world, and now to the precipice of an AI world. And in each era, we valued and leveraged connections to make progress. It was the magic created by teams of people and families that provided the necessary momentum toward community benefit. It was families like the Carnegies and Rockefellers, amongst many, that catalyzed growth for all.

Warren Bennis, in *Organizing Genius*, makes a powerful case that extraordinary achievements are rarely the product of lone geniuses. Instead, they emerge from what he calls "great groups"—teams of people who bring out the best in each other, driven by a shared vision and mutual respect.[2] It's a reminder that human connection isn't just a nice-to-have; it's a force multiplier. The most groundbreaking innovations, the boldest endeavors, and the highest levels of personal achievement often happen not in isolation, but in the presence of others who challenge, support, and inspire us. When we surround ourselves with the right people, those who push us beyond our imagined limits, who question our assumptions, and who fuel our ambitions, we don't just perform better, we become better. Success, at its core, is a collaborative effort, and the most intentional among us know that to go far, we must go together.

When I joined the founding team of Mainspring, we weren't just building a company. We were crafting a movement. John C., a maverick entrepreneur, and our founding team shared an audacious vision: to disrupt the e-commerce strategy consulting world. We weren't just another startup. We were David, preparing to challenge Goliaths like McKinsey and Bain. Our weapon? Not just strategy, but the power of genuine human connection. We didn't recruit employees. We invited dreamers. Top MBA graduates and visionaries who saw beyond spreadsheets to the potential of transformative technology. Our pitch wasn't about salary or titles. It was about community, creativity, and the chance to rewrite industry rules. Two years. Five offices. Three hundred and fifty people. Fifty times revenue growth. A public offering. An acquisition by IBM.

But the true measure of our success wasn't in metrics. It was in the bonds we created. Connections so strong that decades later, we remain a community. We check in. We celebrate each other's progress. We remain curious about each other's evolutions. This is the power of connection: When the right people align around a meaningful mission, they don't just achieve goals. They transform each other. I think that Bennis would agree that success is not an individual sport. It's a collective art.

THE TOPOLOGY OF CONNECTION

Connection is not just about the five people closest to us. That's the core, but human connection extends far beyond our personal circles. We are part of a broader community, a network of interwoven relationships that shape not only our individual lives but also the collective fabric of society. Think about the impact of global movements, from civil rights to climate action. Progress doesn't happen through isolated efforts; it happens when people align their energy toward a common goal. Connection is what fuels these movements. It is why teams outperform individuals, why families form the bedrock of societies, and why communities rise or fall together.

Technology has reshaped how we communicate, but it has not—and cannot—change the fundamental human hunger for genuine connection. We live in an era of infinite digital threads, yet true belonging remains our most profound currency. I think back to the time we lived in Holland when my daughters were young. We were surrounded by tulips, millions of them, each one unique, yet together they created a breathtaking mosaic of color and possibility. That image has stayed with me not just for its beauty, but for what it represented: the power of the collective. But it wasn't just the tulips. It was the people of Holland: their warmth, openness, and willingness to embrace us as their own. They made us feel welcome, like we belonged. We went there temporarily, but their kindness made us want to stay forever. That memory has become a metaphor for the power of human potential: individual brilliance amplified through collective harmony. Living intentionally is not a solitary pursuit. It's a global cultivation, seeding individuals who can transform from isolated tulips into a vibrant field of shared purpose.

My conversations today span continents. With Elle in New Zealand, a youth advocate and changemaker deeply committed to empowering the next generation, I explore how to support young people navigating the uncertainty of emerging adulthood. With KK in South Africa, a visionary educator and guide for "quarter lifers," I imagine building intentional pathways for those hungry for direction, meaning, and hope. These aren't just colleagues; they're cocreators of a mission we all share. They've welcomed me into their local movements and invited me to walk beside them as we bring intentionality to life in communities across the globe. These are not just conversations. They are seeds of a movement. A living, breathing ecosystem of intentional humans who understand that our greatest strength lies in our capacity to support, challenge, and elevate one another. This is bigger than networking. It's something deeper, more human than hashtags, more vital than followers. It's not about scrolling. It's about seeing, *really seeing* each other. It's not about consuming content but creating community. We are writing a new narrative of human potential, one where abundance is not a privilege but a shared birthright; where respect, dreams, and hope are not abstractions, but the scaffolding of a future we're building together.

CONNECTION IN AN AI-DRIVEN WORLD

Now we are entering a new era, one where AI and human connection will intersect in ways we are only beginning to understand. AI will reshape how we connect, but the essence of connection will remain uniquely human. AI will certainly enhance communication. Algorithms will help us identify like-minded people more efficiently. AI-driven platforms will facilitate deeper conversations by suggesting topics of interest and even providing emotional support through advanced natural language processing. Virtual communities will become more sophisticated, blending real-time human interaction with AI-generated insights. But AI cannot replace human connection. Empathy, trust, and vulnerability are fundamentally human traits. The nuance of a shared laugh, the comfort of a reassuring hug, the understanding in a friend's gaze. These are not replicable by algorithms. AI might help facilitate connection, but it cannot replace the heart of it. In fact, as AI becomes more integrated into our lives, human connection will become even more valuable.

When automation takes over transactional tasks, the most essential human skills—caring, creativity, and emotional intelligence—will rise to the forefront. The future of connection won't be about competing with AI; it will be about leveraging AI to deepen and strengthen human bonds. Connection, at its core, is about being seen, understood, and valued. AI may enhance the process, but the outcome, human connection, will always depend on showing up authentically with one another.

Connection is not just about finding the right people—it's about becoming the right person in the presence of others.

SUPPORTING OTHERS STRENGTHENS OUR PURPOSE

One of the most profound ways to strengthen our sense of purpose is through acts of connection and service to others. When we give back, whether through mentoring, volunteering, or simply offering a listening ear, we experience a deep sense of fulfillment that goes beyond personal achievement. Research shows that helping others activates the brain's reward centers, releasing chemicals like dopamine and oxytocin that make us feel good.[3] But beyond the biological response, there's a psychological benefit to giving back. It reminds us that we are all in this together as part of a larger narrative, one that values empathy, compassion, and shared humanity.

I remember coming into the first aid station at the Leadville 100, my first hundred-mile race. My crew greeted me with food and drink, refueled my vest, and sent me off with encouraging words. One of the unique elements of an ultra-marathon over fifty miles is that you can have a crew and pacers to support you and help you get to the finish line, which is no small feat. Your crew becomes a difference-maker. You grow to count on them, and you truly look forward to seeing them at every aid station along the course. I've been so fortunate to have my two daughters, Julianne and Kimberly, as my crew and pacers for most of my hundred-mile races. They are incredible. Julianne takes on the role of crew chief. She meticulously prepares, crafting a detailed plan, gathering whatever I need to eat, and mapping out how to get from one aid station to another. This isn't easy when you're navigating mountains and wild terrain.

On this day, as I traversed the Leadville course, crewing became more challenging as day turned to night and the sunny weather shifted to winter-level cold. The girls did their best to warm me up and keep me moving, but my pace was slowing. Julianne pushed me from mile seventy-five to eighty-seven and urged me to keep moving. At many points, we could hear the buzz of the final aid station in the distance, but it felt like I was going forever, with no aid station in sight. After countless switchbacks and massive boulders to scramble over, we finally reached the last aid station, barely hanging on and only five minutes before the cutoff. That's when Kimberly stepped in to pace me for the last thirteen miles. I was feeling ragged and wondering if I could make it. With my confidence low and the strain of eighty-seven miles in my legs, I stared at the ground, mumbling. Then Kimberly gripped my shoulder, looked me in the eyes, calm, confident, and fierce, and said, "You are going to finish this race. So, let's get going." At that moment, I realized: this wasn't just about me anymore. It was about us.

That's the power of connection. Alone, I might have stopped. But when we show up for each other, when we refuse to let each other quit, we make the impossible possible. Connection isn't just support; it's fuel. I finished the race. I earned the belt buckle. But the real reward was deeper than that. It was the gift and power of connection. When we support each other, we reach places we could never reach alone.

What has surprised me most about this kind of racing is how much I gained from it. The girls gave me the gift of perspective. They reminded me that no one is beyond being supported, and no person is ever truly alone. We find purpose not simply by focusing inward, but by extending our hands to those around us. Connection through supporting each other is a two-way street. As we give, we also receive. We receive gratitude, perspective, and a renewed sense of meaning. Purpose is a living, breathing thing. It grows stronger when shared and deepens when we see its impact on others.

I've come to believe that connection is more than just an emotional need; it's part of our design. We're built for it, not just to survive but to thrive. I may not be a neuroscientist, but I've learned that when we connect with others and show empathy, support, and kindness, something changes in us. Our bodies respond: we feel calmer, more grounded, and more alive. Acts of kindness and service release chemicals in the brain, like dopamine and oxytocin, which reduce stress, deepen trust, and remind us we're not alone. But it's not just biology; it's meaning. When we give of ourselves, we step into purpose. We shift from isolation to contribution, and that change doesn't just help others; it transforms us. It's perspective, it's grace, it's resilience. The more I've leaned into supporting others on and off the race course, the more I've discovered that the greatest rewards come not from pushing harder but from connecting deeper.

PRACTICAL CALL TO ACTION

At my core, I believe we are here to serve. But service doesn't have to mean pacing someone through an ultra-marathon to be meaningful. Opportunities surround us—volunteering at a shelter, mentoring a young professional, or simply checking in on someone who's struggling. Service isn't about recognition or reward. It's about the quiet, profound act of showing up for others. Because in lifting someone else, we often find that we rise too.

Ironically, while true service expects nothing in return, it gives us something invaluable: purpose, connection, and meaning. I've long believed in the "servant leader" model, where leadership and service are not separate but are intertwined. My upbringing and CEO experiences have reinforced that we can both lead and serve, be approachable yet accountable, and create environments where people feel valued. This philosophy aligns with "effective altruism," a movement urging us to be intentional about giving. Not just doing good but doing the *most* good with the resources we have. It pushes us beyond passive generosity into strategic acts of service that can transform lives and communities.

Service isn't about recognition or reward. It's
about the quiet, profound act of showing
up for others. Because in lifting someone
else, we often find that we rise too.

Yet beyond frameworks and strategies, giving is deeply personal. It's about seeing others, understanding their struggles, and stepping in where we can make a difference. My sister Beth, who has led a food pantry for over twenty years, embodies this. She doesn't just distribute food; she builds relationships, offers support in pivotal moments, and leads with unwavering care. Her work reminds me that giving isn't about grand gestures; it's about showing up, again and again, for those who need us.

Purpose is strengthened through action. When we give, we don't just help others; we expand our own capacity for empathy, resilience, and joy. In lifting others, we lift ourselves. The paradox of altruism is that while it seems selfless, it is one of the most rewarding things we can do. So, start today. Find a cause that moves you. Take one step toward service, no matter how small. In doing so, you'll discover that the path to purpose isn't walked alone; it is built through acts of kindness, compassion, and an unwavering commitment to making a difference.

THE POWER OF CONNECTION: MORE THAN JUST A NETWORK

I'm one of those Energizer Bunny kind of people who has touched down in all fifty states and forty-five countries. Not just as a tourist checking boxes, but as someone who can't help but collect people wherever I go. Real connections, not just LinkedIn contacts. The kind of people you can call at three a.m. from another time zone, and they'll actually pick up. So, it wasn't surprising that when I ran six marathons across six continents in six days, I wasn't really on my own. Sure, I did all the running, but I was supported by this incredible web of people who came together to make it possible. Friends showed up at the airports. Strangers became supporters. Someone always had whatever I needed. They didn't just help; they believed in this crazy dream of mine, and their support and belief carried me through from Australia to Los Angeles.

It's funny how connections work; you never really know which ones will change your life. For example, I hired Suzanne, a Cornell grad, and was her manager and mentor at Ernst & Young. She was brilliant and working to find her footing in the corporate world. What nobody told me was how much she'd end up teaching me. Her fresh perspective forced me to question things I'd taken for granted. Her drive made me step up my own game. That's the thing about real connection; it's never just a one-way street.

People talk about networking like it's some kind of strategic game. But in my experience, the most powerful connections happen when we stop trying to network and just start being human. And when we give of ourselves without asking for anything in return, we take it to the next level. I found out that whether I'm crossing the finish line on different continents or helping someone navigate their first year in the corporate world, we're all just people looking for others who get us and want to be part of our unfolding story. And sometimes, when you're lucky, those connections become the invisible threads that hold your biggest adventures together.

HOW DO WE BUILD OUR COLLECTIVE?

Building a strong collective doesn't happen by accident. It requires intentional effort to identify, nurture, and maintain meaningful relationships. Here's how to get started:

1. Be Clear on What You Need:

Reflect on your personal goals. What kind of support do you need to achieve them? Do you need someone to hold you accountable, provide emotional support, or inspire you to think bigger? Knowing what you need will help you recognize the right people to invite into your circle.

2. Seek Out Like-Minded Communities:

If you feel that your current social circle isn't aligned with your growth goals, consider joining new communities. This could be a mastermind group, a professional network, a hobby club, or even online forums focused on personal development.

3. Reach Out and Connect:

Building a collective requires proactive outreach. Reach out to people you admire and respect. Attend events, engage in conversations, and show genuine interest in others. Many people are willing to share their insights and experiences when approached with sincerity and authenticity.

4. Nurture the Relationship:

Relationships thrive on reciprocity. Make a concerted effort to support and uplift those in your circle. Share resources, offer help when needed, and celebrate their successes. When you invest in your collective, it creates a cycle of mutual growth and support.

5. Be Open to Change:

As you evolve, your collective will too. Some relationships may naturally fade, while new ones will emerge. Embrace this change as a natural part of growth.

WHAT TO DO IF YOU FEEL ISOLATED

Not everyone has an immediate network to turn to. If you feel isolated or don't know where to start, consider the following steps:

- **Start Where You Are:** Look at your current surroundings—colleagues, neighbors, community groups. Who stands out as someone you'd like to get to know better?

- **Leverage Online Platforms:** Social media and professional networks like LinkedIn offer opportunities to connect with like-minded individuals from around the world.

- **Join Mastermind or Social Groups:** These groups are designed to bring people together with a shared goal of personal and professional development. I have joined many groups over the past few years, and they are a thread that I pull on from time to time. The Uncharted Group, which I am a member of, is one where I can connect, collaborate, and problem solve across a group of over two thousand entrepreneurs, funders, and innovators.

CHAPTER 9

BE PRESENT EVERY DAY

Living Each Day

We're all time-travelers these days, aren't we? Minds bounce between tomorrow's meetings and yesterday's conversations while bodies stumble through the motions of today. People scroll through social media during dinner, draft emails in their heads during their kids' soccer game, and plan next week's schedule while brushing their teeth. It can feel like this is just how life works in the twenty-first century: waking up to the gentle glow of notifications, sprinting through the day like it's a marathon no one signed up for, and then crashing into bed with minds still racing. Rinse and repeat. But here's the thing about always living in the future or the past: it causes us to miss the only moment we actually have—this one, right now. Being present isn't some mystical state reserved for monks on mountaintops. It doesn't require abandoning goals or pretending deadlines don't exist. It's much simpler than that. Presence is about showing up for life as it's happening.

And when people are fully here, something shifts. Conversations deepen. Colors seem brighter. Even ordinary moments, like waiting for coffee to brew or walking to the car, take on a different quality. Suddenly, they start to notice things: the way sunlight plays on the kitchen counter, the sound of a child's laugh, the feeling of cool air on the skin. Sure, the pings and to-do lists won't disappear. But in the mess of modern life, presence isn't just a nice-to-have; it's a lifeline to what matters most. It's a choice people can make, over and over, to come back to now. To be here. To actually live the life they're so busy planning.

LIVING INTENTIONALLY IN THE NOW

There's a beautiful simplicity in running through the rain, feeling each drop collide with our skin, the wind brushing past our face, the rhythm of our breath syncing with the beat of nature. Yet, there's something about rain that makes us pause. When we get ready to go for a run, a hike, or even a walk, and we glance out the window to see the drops falling from the sky, we hesitate. The rain becomes a barrier, a reason to reconsider our plans. Maybe we change course. Maybe we decide not to go out at all. But what if that hesitation is precisely where the lesson begins?

The rain isn't a blocker; it's where living intentionally actually happens. It's an opportunity to test how we respond to life's unexpected hurdles. That moment of pause, when we have every reason to stay inside, stay dry, and stay comfortable, is the same hesitation we face in countless other moments of life. And the choice we make matters.

Do we let external circumstances dictate our actions, or do we move forward with purpose anyway? Do we allow discomfort to steer us off course, or do we embrace it as part of life? Do we live only when the skies are sunny and the conditions are perfect?

After all these years, I've come to believe something simple yet profound. Life doesn't wait for ideal conditions. It's happening now. In the rain, in the chaos, in the uncertainty. It unfolds in the middle of a messy house, a tough conversation, or a turbulent market. Maybe our greatest opportunity isn't in avoiding the hard stuff but in meeting it head-on. Maybe the tough conditions aren't obstacles to the experience; maybe they *are* the experience. The rain soaks us, wakes us up, and pulls us into the present. And the more we step into those moments, the more we discover this is where life really happens.

I've spent two decades learning to love what others call "bad" weather. The worse it gets, the more it calls to me. While others retreat, I've learned to lean into the howling winds before a hurricane, the bitter cold that freezes your eyelashes, and the crushing heat that makes your blood feel like it's boiling. These aren't just weather conditions, they're experiences that expand the boundaries of what we think is possible. Think about it. We all know what it feels like to sit in a climate-controlled office or a cozy living room. But how many people know the sharp sting of sleet against their cheeks during a winter storm, or the way thunder feels in their chest while perched on a hillside watching lightning dance across the sky? These moments become the stories we tell, the memories that stand out in the endless parade of comfortable, forgettable days.

This isn't about some social media-worthy challenge or a trendy lifestyle hashtag. Ask any Navy SEAL about being comfortable with discomfort, and they'll tell you it's what keeps them alive. They maintain peak performance because they've learned to see past the noise, the rain, the crowds, and the chaos to focus on what really matters. Living intentionally means finding that signal through the noise and acting on it, regardless of the conditions around us.

So many people get stuck waiting for the secret to living intentionally to reveal itself. They sit in that waiting room of life, wondering when the answer will arrive. But what's been staring us in the face all along is this: living intentionally isn't a destination, it's the journey itself. It's in the moments when we choose to step out into the rain instead of watching it from behind glass. It's embracing the discomfort, the uncertainty, and the imperfect conditions that life presents us. Learning to love the rain, both the literal drops and the metaphorical storms, means choosing to be fully present in every moment, not just the easy ones. It means understanding that life is happening right now, whether we're ready for it or not. This is the foundation of living intentionally, of being present every day. The storm isn't something to wait out; it's an invitation to truly live.

EMBRACING THE EDGE OF BEING PRESENT

We all talk about getting out of our comfort zone. But when was the last time you chose discomfort? Not because life forced your hand, but because something inside you whispered, "This is where growth lives." After two decades of public speaking, from intimate boardrooms to packed auditoriums, I thought I had mastered discomfort. I'd learned to embrace the butterflies in my stomach. The nervous energy before taking the stage had become an old friend. But confidence is sneaky, it wraps you in a warm blanket of competence until you forget what it feels like to truly push your limits.

That's why, when the opportunity came to coproduce the *Ageless Living* series for PBS, I knew I had to do something radical. This wasn't just another speaking engagement. It was bigger than that. My words would be broadcast into homes across the country, preserved on film alongside fifteen other talks, all of them set to live forever. No pressure, right? One late night, during a brainstorming session with Dana and Kelly (my collaborators on the series), they threw out a suggestion so wild it stopped me cold.

"You should rap. On stage. In front of hundreds of people."

I laughed, assuming they were joking.

"I'm not—I can barely—I don't even know who Eminem is," I stammered.

But they weren't backing down. Dana laid down a beat on his keyboard. Kelly started scribbling lyrics. Suddenly, the rap was taking shape right there in front of me, and something electric filled the room. My heart was racing, and I couldn't tell if it was fear or excitement. Probably both. But in that moment, sitting in their studio, watching this crazy idea come to life, I knew the answer.

"I'll do it."

The next few weeks were a blur of preparation. My car became a mobile rehearsal studio. Hotel rooms transformed into secret practice spaces. Every red light was a chance to run through lines. I'd catch glimpses of myself in mirrors, baseball cap sideways, trying to find a rhythm that still felt foreign on my tongue. Each session was a tug-of-war between determination and doubt. What if I froze? What if the audience saw this as a man in a midlife crisis instead of a message about growth?

Then came the moment.

The PBS filming was going perfectly. My talk flowed. The audience was engaged. Then...the lights went black. The theater went silent. And in those first few moments of darkness, I had transformed. When the beat dropped, the lights came up to reveal something no one expected: me in a hoodie, sunglasses, and a sideways cap, a costume that felt both ridiculous and absolutely necessary.

Boom. Boom. Boom.

The bass kicked in, syncing with my heartbeat. Mic in hand, I was either going to crash and burn or create something unforgettable. "Yo, yo, yo, I got a story to tell," I began, my voice steady despite the earthquake inside, "about how I created THPL. The High Performance Life is the way I roll; it gives me a feeling of purpose and soul."

Time blurred. I was inside the moment and watching it from above at the same time. The audience's faces shifted, from confusion to surprise to something deeper. Recognition, maybe. Of their own battles with fear. With discomfort.

When I finished, I dropped the mic. It wasn't planned, but it felt perfect. A punctuation mark on one of the most vulnerable moments of my life. The audience erupted, cheers mixed with gasps of disbelief. Slowly, I pulled off the sunglasses, stepping back into my everyday persona. "Now you know," I said, voice thick with emotion, "what it feels like to feel comfortable while being uncomfortable." At that moment, drenched in sweat and adrenaline, I realized I hadn't just delivered a memorable performance. I had *lived* the message. Growth doesn't just happen beyond the comfort zone; it *thrives* in the moments when we choose to be spectacularly, authentically vulnerable.[1]

There's something powerful about declaring our intentions to the world; it makes us feel very present. Public goals create an electric tension between possibility and vulnerability. The moment we say it out loud, "This is what I'm going to do," we cross a threshold. There's no hiding anymore. They know. We know. We are truly in the moment. Sure, the doubts creep in: "What if I fail? What if I never start? Will people remember my bold declaration?" But these very questions, this dance with discomfort, are exactly what pushes us toward breakthrough moments. I certainly learned this firsthand when I stepped up to perform my rap. Each performance, from the first nervous delivery to the confident final show, pushed me through layers of vulnerability into a space of pure presence and intention. I wasn't just performing; I was rewiring my relationship with risk and commitment and learning how to be present. This is how we build our commitment muscle—the ability to make promises and keep them, not just to others, but to ourselves. Every time we follow through, we reinforce that we are capable and intentional. It's not about perfection; it's about presence. About showing up fully for the moments we create.

Take my daily blog, for instance. For over 4,500 consecutive days, I've sat down, no matter where I was or how I felt, to think, write, edit, and share. People often ask when I'll stop or why I continue. But that question misses the point. Why do we frame life in terms of stopping? Why is endurance seen as something that must eventually expire? The truth is, I have no plan to stop. This blog is part of who I am. It's not a task, it's a rhythm, a ritual. Of course, I've become a better writer. But that's not why I do it. I do it because it brings me back to the present. Because it anchors me in intention. Each post is a small act of mindfulness, a quiet vow to show up for myself, regardless of mood or circumstance.

Over the years, this practice has shaped me in ways I couldn't have foreseen. Looking back, it's clear that this book wasn't born from a single moment of inspiration; it was carved slowly, one entry at a time, like water shaping stone. It didn't come in a flash. It came through thousands of intentional choices. That's the quiet truth about presence: it's forged in the small, private moments when no one's watching. We don't rise to a challenge by accident. We rise to the level of our preparation. The blog, for me, was never about going viral; it was about building a foundation. A muscle of commitment. A pattern of showing up.

So, when life hands us a stage, a promotion, a crisis, a crossroads, we don't suddenly become capable. We reveal the capacity we've been building all along. And when that foundation is solid, fear begins to lose its grip. Because in the end, it's not about the outcome. It's about the integrity of our effort. How we show up. How we hold the line. How we honor the promise we've made to ourselves—not to be perfect, but to be present. Both Buddhist and Stoic teachings remind us that attachment to outcomes is the root of suffering. When we release that grip, when we stop measuring the value of life by results alone—the likes, the views, the clicks—we create space for something deeper. We become less entangled in fear and more rooted in purpose. We experience life not as a series of finish lines to cross, but as a way of being. The blog, the run, the speech, the hard day at work, they become not means to an end, but expressions of who we are. That's where meaning lives. In the doing, not the proving. In the quiet, consistent practice of showing up, especially when no one is watching.

Remember running in the rain? Making the hard phone call? Having the conversation you wanted to avoid? These aren't footnotes in life; they're the training ground. And when we meet those moments with full presence, something powerful happens; we come alive. The discomfort becomes the teacher. The resistance becomes the reveal. We stop seeing ourselves as someone merely surviving the storm and start seeing who we are because of it. This is the path from ordinary to extraordinary, not through grand, sweeping gestures, but through a thousand grounded choices. Living intentionally isn't about side-stepping the hard parts of life. It's about learning to meet them with courage and clarity. It's about waking up each day with curiosity instead of fear, presence instead of distraction. We don't wait to feel inspired to show up—we show up, and inspiration follows. Presence isn't a side effect of ease; it's a product of discipline. And discipline, lived daily and anchored in our heart, becomes intention.

MINDFULNESS MATTERS

Mindfulness is the tool that helps us practice presence. It's a simple concept: paying attention, on purpose, in the present moment, without judgment. But simple doesn't mean easy. Our minds naturally want to drift to the past or project into the future. Practicing mindfulness means gently guiding our attention back to the now, repeatedly, like returning to our breath during meditation. Dr. Ellen Langer, a renowned Harvard psychologist, has extensively explored the concepts of mindfulness and mindlessness. Over the years, she has highlighted that mindfulness is the simple act of actively noticing new things. When we do this, it puts us in the present, makes us sensitive to context, and it's literally and figuratively enlivening. Most people think they're aware, but they're not. Langer's work suggests that mindfulness isn't about meditation but about actively engaging with life. Her research shows that when we shift from autopilot (mindlessness) to awareness (mindfulness), we unlock greater potential, performance, and well-being.[2]

Why does this matter? Mindfulness allows us to engage more deeply with life and to be fully present. When we're mindful, we notice the little things: the way light dances through the trees, the hum of laughter in a coffee shop, the solid feel of the earth beneath our feet. We don't just move through life, we savor it. We make wiser choices, not from a place of stress or reactivity, but from grounded awareness. We respond with clarity, not impulse. And in doing so, we create space for better decisions, deeper connections, and a more intentional way of being.

> We make wiser choices, not from a place of stress or reactivity, but from grounded awareness. We respond with clarity, not impulse. And in doing so, we create space for better decisions, deeper connections, and a more intentional way of being.

We often hear phrases like "live in the moment" or "be present," but what does that truly mean? It's more than just a catchy mantra. It's about recognizing that life only ever happens in the present moment. The past is a memory; the future is a dream. The only thing we have control over is right now. And yet, so many of us live anywhere but in the present. We dwell on past mistakes, replaying them in our minds like a broken record. Or we project into the future, worrying about things that may never happen. Meanwhile, the present moment, the only place where life happens, slips by unnoticed. Mindfulness doesn't mean ignoring the past or neglecting future planning. It means acknowledging those things without letting them consume us. And when contemplating the past or planning for the future, we are aware of what we are doing. It's about being fully alive in the now, appreciating what we have, and making the most of each moment.

To live intentionally means to show up for our life every single day. It means embracing each moment, even the uncomfortable ones. Especially the uncomfortable ones. Because that's where growth happens. When we do this, we get on the track from ordinary to extraordinary.

WHEN TIME DISAPPEARS

We've all experienced flow or at least heard of it. That effortless, hyper-focused state where time seems to slow down, distractions disappear, and we feel completely immersed in the moment. This is flow state, a concept that psychologist Mihaly Csikszentmihalyi spent his life trying to understand.[3] It's not just some feel-good phenomenon; it's the secret weapon of human potential. Think about the last time you were so absorbed in something that you forgot to eat. Maybe you were painting and suddenly, the sun was setting. Or you were writing, and those three hours felt like minutes. That's not just focus, it's your brain functioning in its most optimal state. Flow isn't merely about feeling good; it's about accessing parts of ourselves that usually remain hidden. When we're in flow, our brain waves shift. Our neurochemistry changes. We process information differently. The inner critic—that nagging voice of self-doubt—goes quiet. In its place comes a profound sense of capability, of rightness, of being exactly where we need to be.

But what makes flow truly remarkable is that it is not just for artists or athletes. It's not reserved for meditation masters or musical prodigies. Flow is deeply democratic. It's available to anyone who puts themselves in the position to access it. A parent playing with their child can find it. A gardener tending their plants can slip into it. A programmer solving a complex problem can ride its currents.

Steven Kotler, who's spent decades studying flow at the Flow Research Collective, puts it this way: flow isn't just an optimal state of consciousness, it's a gateway to what humans are truly capable of. When we're in flow, we're not just better at what we do; we're better at who we are. We're more creative, more decisive, more present. Research suggests we're up to five times more productive, but that almost misses the point.[4] The real magic isn't in what flow helps us produce, it's in how it helps us evolve. For as much as we fully understand human consciousness, flow stands as perhaps its purest expression. It's what happens when we align our actions with our deepest intentions, when we find that sweet spot between challenge and skill, when we're fully present in our lives rather than just passing through them. In flow, we're not trying to live intentionally; we simply are.

> When we're in flow, we're not just better at
> what we do; we're better at who we are. We're
> more creative, more decisive, more present.

The beauty of flow is that it can be cultivated. Like a muscle, our ability to enter flow states grows stronger with practice. It starts with creating the right conditions: clear goals, immediate feedback, and the right level of challenge. But it goes deeper than that. Flow requires trust—in ourselves, in the process, in the moment. It asks us to release our death grip on control and allow ourselves to be carried by something larger than our everyday concerns. Each time we enter flow, we learn something about what truly engages us, what challenges us in the right ways, and what makes time disappear.

I've found that sense of time dissolving most vividly when I write. Not always at first, sometimes the page stares back, blank and unbothered, the cursor blinking like a dare. One of my favorite blog posts is called "The Blank Page" because, in the moment, it feels like an ending. But it turns out to be a beginning, a bridge into flow. That moment taught me something essential: if I stay with the discomfort long enough, something always shifts. A phrase lands. An idea opens. And suddenly I'm no longer writing *from* my mind; I'm writing *through* it, from someplace deeper. The noise quiets. The edges blur. Time becomes elastic, and the words feel less like effort and more like remembering. In those moments, I'm not chasing insight. I *am* insight. Flow strips away everything artificial and leaves behind only what is real. And in that purity, I'm reminded why I write, not just to create, but to connect. With myself. With others. With what truly matters. Looking back now, it's clear how prescient that post was. A quiet reminder that when we show up again and again, something in us keeps evolving. Here's what I wrote:

The Blank Page

Every day I sit down to write, I begin with a blank page. No agenda. No roadmap. Just the cursor blinking like a dare. It could feel daunting, but it has become a sacred ritual. Because I've learned that what looks like emptiness is possibility. It's a canvas for clarity, creativity, and courage. Each post I've written, each insight I've uncovered, came not from knowing in advance but from the commitment to begin. The blank page has taught me that flow doesn't come from waiting for the perfect idea. It comes from showing up. From trusting the process. From believing that something meaningful will rise

if I just start. And that's true not just in writing but in life.
We all face blank pages. The question is: Will we fill them?

That's the quiet gift of flow. It doesn't demand perfection; it invites presence. It rewards those who show up with intention, and it carries those who are willing to let go of control. In the end, flow reveals that our best life isn't built through force of will alone, but through a dance between discipline and surrender, between effort and ease. In flow, time loses its grip on us. Minutes stretch into hours, and hours collapse into moments. Effort feels like play; work becomes art. Ideas connect like lightning. Decisions come with clarity and ease. Our productivity doesn't just improve; it transcends. But the true gift of flow isn't in what we get done. It's in how we feel while doing it: fully present, deeply alive, and unmistakably aligned with something greater.

TUNING THE BRAIN: DESIGNING FLOW IN THE BRAIN

As performance researcher Steven Kotler explains, flow isn't mystical; it's measurable. Flow has distinct biological markers, and understanding them gives us tools to *intentionally* access our best selves. Just as we train our bodies, we can train our minds to enter that state of deep presence, creativity, and focus with more consistency. And at the heart of this is presence—that is, the ability to be fully here, fully engaged, fully alive.

When we enter flow, something remarkable happens under the surface. The brain shifts into a hyper-efficient mode that affects our chemistry, cognition, and consciousness. It begins with a neurochemical cocktail. Dopamine, endorphins, and anandamide flood the brain, elevating mood, sharpening attention, and enhancing pattern recognition. Simultaneously, the prefrontal cortex, the part responsible for self-monitoring, doubt, and time tracking, quiets down. This is why flow feels so free: we're no longer overthinking, second-guessing, or watching the clock. Finally, the brain transitions from fast-moving beta waves into slower alpha and theta waves, the same frequencies associated with deep meditation and REM sleep. In flow, we are calm but highly alert, intensely focused but deeply relaxed. We're not just more productive; we're more ourselves.[5]

HOW TO TRIGGER FLOW

Flow rarely happens by accident. It's most often the result of conditions we *intentionally* create. Researchers like Steven Kotler and Mihaly Csikszentmihalyi have identified specific triggers that help us enter flow more reliably, and the formula is surprisingly accessible. Flow happens when challenge meets skill just beyond our comfort zone. We're stretched but not overwhelmed. The brain thrives on this sweet spot; it's what keeps us engaged, focused, and curious.

Here's how to create your own gateway into flow:

Find the Challenge/Skill Sweet Spot

Choose a task that's just slightly outside your current skill level, around 5–10 percent harder. It's the edge of your capability that activates engagement.

Eliminate Distractions

Block ninety minutes of focused time. Silence notifications, close extra tabs, and clear your environment of interruptions. Better yet, turn off your phone and put it away. Deep work requires deep space.

Build a Pre-Flow Ritual

Cue your brain that it's time to focus. Try a few minutes of resonant breathing, a short meditation, or listening to instrumental music. The ritual creates the runway.

Set a Clear, Time-Bound Goal

Instead of "I'll work on my project," say "I'll finish the first draft in the next two hours." Flow thrives on clarity.

Recover Intentionally

After 90–120 minutes of focused work, take a purposeful break. Walk outside, stretch, and breathe. Recovery isn't optional; it's fuel for your next flow cycle.

By designing our mindset, space, and energy with intention, we can access flow not occasionally, but as a regular rhythm in how we live, create, and perform.

PRESENCE IS THE GATEWAY TO FLOW

Flow may be the peak state, but presence is the gateway. And staying present in a world of pings, dings, and constant distraction is its own kind of superpower. We're constantly toggling between fight-or-flight and rest-and-digest. Our nervous system reacts to every input, real or imagined. Presence helps us rebalance. It's the practice of returning to this moment. Not the worry of the future or the noise of the past, but the now. And the most powerful entry point is breath.

Use Your Breath to Anchor the Moment

One of the simplest, most powerful tools is box breathing, a technique used by Navy SEALs and high performers alike. Inhale for four counts. Hold for four. Exhale for four. Hold again for four. Repeat. This pattern regulates the nervous system, sharpens focus, and grounds you in the present. You can use it before a big meeting, during a challenging workout, or when you simply feel scattered. The breath is always there, and so is the reset.

Create Rituals That Ground You

Rituals help transform presence into a daily practice. They don't have to be elaborate, just consistent. A few quiet minutes with your coffee in the morning. An evening walk without your phone. A moment of gratitude before bed. These small, sacred habits become the scaffolding of an intentional life.

Turn Discomfort into Practice

Presence isn't just about peace; it's also about discomfort. When we stop resisting what's hard and instead stay with it—rain on our skin, a difficult conversation, a workout that pushes us—we build the muscle of presence. Life doesn't only happen when it's easy. It happens when we choose to be there for all of it.

PRESENCE PRACTICES TO TRY

Presence is the price of admission to a meaningful life. It's how we enter flow, find our reality, and live intentionally. And the beautiful part? You don't need permission. You don't need more time. You don't need to be perfect. You just need to begin. Right here, right now.

Here are a few simple rituals to bring you back to the moment:

- **Mindful Morning:** Before reaching for your phone, sit quietly for five minutes. Breathe. Set an intention for the day. Express gratitude for something, anything.

- **Presence Check-ins:** Set a subtle reminder to pause three times a day. Ask: "Where is my attention right now?" Then gently bring it back to the now.

- **Reflect at Night:** Before bed, note three moments when you felt truly present. And three things you're grateful for. This helps wire your brain for mindfulness.

- **Embrace the Elements:** Next time it rains, go outside. Feel it. Let it remind you that life is always happening, right here, right now.

CHAPTER 10

THE RIPPLE EFFECT

Ripples in the Water

A skipped stone on a quiet pond, sometimes it takes something so simple to remind us of our impact. One small stone, barely the size of a coin, can wake up an entire body of water. The ripples stretch outward, unseen and unstoppable, touching shores we may never reach. So, it is with our actions. Every word spoken, every gesture of kindness, every moment of vulnerability. We are casting stones into the world. And though we may never witness the full reach of those ripples, they matter. They shape stories. They change lives. Think of the last time someone was moved by your presence. Maybe it was a friend who felt heard. Or a stranger lifted by your unexpected kindness. We rarely see how far our influence travels, but it does. The ripple reached them. We all carry these stones. The question is: What kind of ripples are you creating?

THE POWER OF A SINGLE ACT

We tend to underestimate the power of a single act, especially our own. Maybe it's humility. Maybe it's comfort. Maybe it's the belief that impact is the province of others—those who are louder, bigger, more important. But when we live intentionally, we quietly step out of that mindset. We begin to show up, not with grand gestures, but with consistent presence. And that's where the shift happens. Because intentional living doesn't just change *us*; it changes the people around us. The ripple starts there. With a kind word. A brave decision. A shared story. When we live with purpose, our actions, whether bold or seemingly small, create waves that reach beyond us, influencing others in ways we may never fully see or comprehend.

> When we live with purpose, our actions, whether
> bold or seemingly small, create waves that
> reach beyond us, influencing others in ways
> we may never fully see or comprehend.

Like a pebble dropped into still water, our actions carry more weight than we realize. The ripples may be quiet, even invisible to us, but they move. They travel through conversations, through relationships, and through time. What we learn is that we don't need a platform or a following to create change. We just need to be present. To live in alignment with what we believe. The impact doesn't come from size; it comes from sincerity. One voice. One act. One moment of courage can be enough to shift someone's course. And sometimes, if we're lucky, we get to witness just how far those ripples have traveled.

In today's fast-paced, hyper-connected world, it may feel harder than ever to make a meaningful impact. The sheer volume of voices, opinions, and distractions can seem to drown out our efforts to live a life of significance. But the reality is that the ripple effect works quietly and persistently, often outside of our immediate awareness. It starts with us, with our willingness to be intentional, to live authentically, and to show up in ways that matter. And every once in a while, life reminds us just how far our ripples can travel. An email arrived in my inbox on a typical Tuesday morning: "You might not remember me, but we worked together 15 years ago." My coffee paused halfway to my lips as I read Lauren's message. "I felt a strong connection with you then and have been following you since. Your message and way of living really resonate with me. Would you be willing to spend 30 minutes with me to talk about the career transition I'm going through?" Fifteen years. No contact. Just silence and distance and time, until this moment, when something I'd done or said back then, something I probably didn't even think twice about, had slowly drifted back to me across the waters to reach out and tap me on the shoulder.

"Absolutely, I would love to reconnect," I wrote back immediately.

Our Zoom call felt like opening a time capsule, but with a new perspective layered on old memories. We covered more ground in thirty minutes than some people manage in hours. Later that day, Lauren's follow-up message landed in my inbox: "Thank you for your time today. It was incredibly gracious of you to take my call. Your perspective is fascinating and motivating. It inspires me to think differently about my own path." I sat with that message for a while, letting its weight sink in. Here's what struck me: we're all throwing stones into the water every single day. The way we treat people, the energy we bring to conversations, the values we choose to live by, they're all creating ripples. But unlike actual ripples on a pond, these don't fade away after a few seconds. They can travel for years, decades even, touching lives in ways we may never see. Lauren reminded me that being a role model isn't about doing anything special or extraordinary. It's about living authentically and consistently, guided by values like respect, gratitude, and integrity. That's all someone needs to see: someone else walking their talk, day after day, to find their way forward. Years later, those ripples come back to remind us that everything we do matters. Everything.

For me, it has not stopped there. I regularly receive messages from subscribers of my blog about a post I'd written that helped them make a difficult decision. When I wrote the post, I did not have a specific intended action, but it caused action in the life of one of my readers. That's the thing about ripples; they travel further than we ever know. We touch lives in ways we may never hear about. But that doesn't make the impact any less real. That's what keeps me writing, keeps me sharing, keeps me showing up, not for recognition, but for resonance.

> That's the thing about ripples; they travel further
> than we ever know. We touch lives in ways we
> may never hear about. But that doesn't make
> the impact any less real. That's what keeps me
> writing, keeps me sharing, keeps me showing
> up, not for recognition, but for resonance.

More broadly, remember Greta Thunberg? In 2018, she was a seemingly normal fifteen-year-old girl sitting alone outside the Swedish

Parliament with a handmade sign. Her solitary "School Strike for Climate" wasn't meant to spark a global movement. She was simply acting on her convictions: quietly, intentionally. And yet, that single act of purpose ignited something powerful. Today, millions of young people around the world have joined her cause. Greta's story demonstrates the profound impact that living intentionally can have. Her action, authentic and aligned with her values, demonstrated that even the smallest stone, when dropped with conviction, can create waves that reshape the shoreline.

BECOMING A ROLE MODEL–
WHETHER WE REALIZE IT OR NOT

"I started running because of you."

The message caught me off guard. It was from Steve, a colleague I had worked closely with. Apparently, he'd been listening to me talk about my daily run, day after day, rain or shine. He never mentioned it at the time. But there he was, now asking for a plan to run his first marathon. Influence often works quietly. We don't set out to be someone's inspiration. We simply live our lives, make our choices, and somewhere along the way, we find ourselves woven into someone else's story.

You don't need to lead a revolution or give TED talks to create meaningful change. The most powerful ripples often start with the smallest actions. It could be as simple as a parent choosing to put down their phone during dinner, showing their children what real connection looks like. A team member admitting they made a mistake permits others to be human. A friend setting healthy boundaries demonstrates what self-respect looks like in practice. These moments matter because they're real. They're accessible. They show people that change isn't some distant, impossible dream; it's something that happens in ordinary moments, through ordinary choices. I think about these examples of unsolicited feedback that I have received:

> *"Thank you for the push and motivation! I'm loving it."*
> —Melica

> *"I've been watching the videos you've posted recently. They've inspired a ton of contemplation for me—I think they'll do the same for others."*—Whitney

> *"It was an inspirational conversation. I'm working on a plan for this year of what I want to do for 365 days, how I am going to hold myself accountable, and how I can use that to build a platform to share it with people."*—Brendan

> *"Congrats on beating your 150,000 push-up goal. I frequently do a handful of push-ups a day to strengthen my back— but you've inspired me to make that an intentional, daily goal."*—Kristen

> *"You are a paragon of health and fitness—and are an inspiration to me."*—Joel

> *"I would love to learn more about you; you truly inspired me!"*—Shane

These messages humble me. They remind me that we're all walking billboards for our values, whether we intend to be or not. Every choice we make, how we spend our time, how we treat others, and how we treat ourselves, sends a message about what we believe is possible and permissible in life. This isn't about the pressure to be perfect. It's about understanding that our lives naturally overflow into others'. When we choose to live with intention, to align our actions with our values, we create a permission slip for others to do the same. We become living proof that different choices are possible.

> Influence often works quietly. We don't set out to be someone's inspiration. We simply live our lives, make our choices, and somewhere along the way, we find ourselves woven into someone else's story.

Think about a time you had a positive impact on someone's life, even in a small way. Maybe you encouraged them, helped them see something differently, or simply showed up when they needed it. Or think about a time someone told you that your example inspired them. Those moments matter more than we realize.

SOMETIMES THE QUIETEST CHOICES CREATE THE LOUDEST RIPPLES

My father never made a big show about not cursing. He simply didn't do it. No dramatic stands, no lectures about morality, just a quiet commitment to speaking with respect. Growing up, I watched how he navigated frustrating moments without resorting to four-letter words, how he expressed himself clearly and powerfully without falling back on profanity. It wasn't weakness; it was intentional strength.

When I entered the professional world, I carried this legacy with me. In conference rooms and casual conversations, in moments of stress and celebration, I chose my words carefully. Not out of prudishness, but out of respect for the example my father had set. I never announced this choice or asked others to follow suit. I simply lived it. What happened next surprised me. Conversations would clean themselves up, not because anyone had to, but because they chose to. I'd hear colleagues mid-curse and watch them catch themselves. "Oh, sorry about that!" they'd say with a slight smile. These moments always touched me, not because I minded the cursing, but because it showed how one person's quiet commitment could ripple out to influence others' choices.

The pattern played out again and again, usually after a few months of working together, someone would ask: "I've noticed you never swear. Why is that?" When I'd explain about my dad, about carrying forward his values, something beautiful would happen. Their faces would soften. "That's cool," they'd say, often followed by a story about their own parents' values, or something they hoped to pass on to their kids. What started as a simple question about word choice would open deeper conversations about legacy, respect, and the values we choose to live by.

My dad's influence didn't just stop with me; it created new ripples in conference rooms and offices he'd never set foot in, touching conversations he'd never be part of. That's the magic of living your values quietly but consistently. You don't need to preach or persuade. You just need to be steady in your commitments, clear in your choices, and the ripples will spread on their own.

We all have these opportunities, these chances to stand for something. Maybe it's about language, or integrity, or how we treat others under pressure. The specific choice matters less than the consistency with which we honor it. When we hold true to our standards, not with rigidity but with quiet conviction, people notice. More importantly, they respect it. Not because we demanded that respect, but because we earned it through our actions. In the end, my father's legacy lives on not just in my choices but in the subtle shifts in the people I interact with. It's a reminder that our values, lived authentically day after day, can create ripples that travel far beyond our own circles, touching lives we may never know about.

> You don't need to preach or persuade. You just need to be steady in your commitments, clear in your choices, and the ripples will spread on their own.

Sometimes the ripples we create are obvious, like when someone directly tells us we've influenced them. But more often, they're invisible to us, spreading outward in ways we may never know about. That's both the beauty and the responsibility of it: we're always teaching something by the way we live, whether we mean to or not. The question isn't whether we'll be a role model. The question is what kind of role model we'll be.

> We're always teaching something by the way we live, whether we mean to or not. The question isn't whether we'll be a role model. The question is what kind of role model we'll be.

VULNERABILITY IN LEADERSHIP

Think about the leaders who have had the biggest impact on you. Were they the ones who always had the right answers and never showed weakness? Or were they the ones who admitted when they were wrong, asked for help when they needed it, and treated you like a human being rather than just an employee?

What we learn is that vulnerability in leadership isn't a weakness; it's a strength. Leaders who are willing to admit mistakes, seek input, and acknowledge challenges create stronger, more resilient teams. Employees are more likely to trust leaders who demonstrate vulnerability because it shows humanity and relatability. It sends the message that it's okay to be imperfect and that growth comes from learning through experiences. And every time we lead with vulnerability and authenticity, we create a ripple effect. When a leader admits a mistake or asks for help, it permits others to do the same. Trust builds. Collaboration deepens. Resilience grows. The ripples of one act of vulnerability can reshape the culture of an entire team or organization.

I remember early in my career taking a leadership course with John Kotter, the Harvard thought leader on change and leadership. He showed us contrasting examples of leadership from Eastern Airlines and Southwest Airlines, and the ripple effects of different leadership styles couldn't have been starker. Eastern Airlines was struggling. At the time, CEO Frank Borman recorded a video blaming the employees for the company's poor performance. The message was clear: *you're the problem.* It created a ripple effect of defensiveness and fear throughout the organization. Employees became hesitant to take risks or innovate because they feared being blamed for failure. In contrast, Herb Kelleher, the CEO of Southwest Airlines, took the opposite approach. He recorded a video thanking his employees for their cooperation, resilience, and support for each other. He highlighted that this positive, gracious attitude was Southwest's true competitive advantage.

The outcome? Eastern Airlines filed for bankruptcy; Southwest went on to forty-seven straight years of profitability.

The lesson was clear: the ripples we create as leaders, whether through blame or gratitude, shape the culture and future of the organization. Vulnerability and humility are not soft skills; they are strategic tools for long-term success. Leadership creates cultural ripples that determine whether an organization thrives or collapses. Frank Borman's leadership at Eastern Airlines created all the wrong ripples, eroding trust, suppressing creativity, and ultimately contributing to the company's downfall. In contrast, Herb Kelleher's leadership at Southwest Airlines created a different kind of ripple, one built on trust, innovation, and resilience, which led to decades of profitability. We don't always see the ripples we create in the moment. But make no mistake, our vulnerability (or lack of it) sets a tone that others will follow.

THE RIPPLE EFFECT OF VULNERABILITY

Being vulnerable can be hard. The more vulnerable, the higher the perceived risk, which translates to a world where vulnerability can affect mental health. In a society where social media often promotes curated highlights, it's easy to feel isolated by our struggles. Public companies are flogged for minor strays from expectations. We are told to be strong, not weak, and to block out our emotions because they're not what people expect from us. But that's not how humans work. We are hardwired for connection. And vulnerability, not perfection, is the foundation of trust. When individuals openly share their challenges, whether it's dealing with anxiety, failure, or personal loss, it normalizes these experiences. It reduces the stigma around vulnerability and creates a culture of support and empathy. It frees us all to be better versions of ourselves because we are not using false pretenses or phony representations to rob us of our energy. Vulnerability creates a ripple effect that extends from one conversation, one moment of honesty, into the culture and relationships around us.

I've experienced this firsthand. Early in my career, I thought that to lead effectively, I needed to always project strength, to have all the answers, and to never show weakness. It was apparent that all we did was celebrate the wins, the highlights, and the achievements, but we rarely talked about the struggle underneath. I quickly learned that this created distance between me and my team. If, indeed, struggle is where the growth happens, then I was going to need to admit that I didn't have all the answers, that I could use their help. Then real trust began to form. The moment I was willing to be vulnerable, I noticed my team members doing the same. They began to ask more questions, propose new ideas, and support each other more openly. That's the power of the ripple effect. One act of vulnerability gives others permission to lean into their own authenticity, reduces shame, builds support, and strengthens communities.

I've seen this play out in my own life. I have had the opportunity to be on stage telling my story of my less-than-ordinary start to my adulthood. I describe how I didn't have a date until halfway through college, and I wasn't invited to any of the "cool kids'" parties, or any parties, for that matter. I so desperately wanted to be included, but as hard as I wanted it, it just didn't come. That was until I reframed my situation, realizing that if I wanted to go to a party, all I had to do was host one and invite others to attend. It worked. I threw a lot of parties, and I finally had the fun and connection I was looking for.

But the real ripple effect happened afterward. When I shared this story on stage, the vulnerability I showed created a wave of connection. After stepping off the stage, people would come up to me and say, "I wasn't invited to the parties either!" We would laugh and acknowledge that in the long run, it wasn't a tragedy, but the shared experience made us feel more connected. That moment of openness created a ripple of belonging. It made others feel seen and understood. Vulnerability doesn't just open doors; it opens hearts. By sharing my experience, I gave others permission to reflect on their own stories and realize that they weren't alone. That's what happens when we are vulnerable: it normalizes struggle, dismantles shame, and builds connection. And vulnerability enhances resilience. By acknowledging and confronting our struggles, we build the emotional tools to navigate future challenges more effectively. Vulnerability teaches us that we are not defined by our failures but by how we rise above them. It transforms pain into power and hardship into strength. The ripples we create, through vulnerability, honesty, and connection, shape not only our own lives but the lives of those around us. Vulnerability is contagious. When you lead with honesty and courage, you create ripples that inspire others to step into their own authenticity.

By acknowledging and confronting our struggles, we build the emotional tools to navigate future challenges more effectively. Vulnerability teaches us that we are not defined by our failures but by how we rise above them.

THE RIPPLE ALWAYS HAPPENS

Without a doubt, it's fun to tell my story of running six marathons on six continents in six days. I tell it because I appreciate hearing stories like it. It's unique and different, and some interesting insights came from that once-in-a-lifetime experience. But I don't tell it to inspire people, at least, not directly. I tell it because it was a personal test of endurance, resilience, and growth. It was about proving to myself that I could push through discomfort and challenge to achieve something extraordinary. Yet, the ripple effect happens whether I intend it or not.

After sharing the story, I am almost always contacted by a friend or an acquaintance who tells me their own story of a challenge they had wanted to take on for so long, and how hearing about my adventure gave them the motivation to finally go after it. That goal they had previously deemed impossible was achieved. They pushed past their own limits. One friend reached out after hearing my story and told me how they had always wanted to train for a marathon but had been too intimidated to start. Hearing about my six-marathon challenge made them realize that they were capable of more than they gave themselves credit for. They signed up for a race, trained hard, and finished, proving to themselves that they were stronger than they thought. It's humbling to know that my story created a ripple effect, sparking action and change in someone else's life. I'm not sure what could be better than being part of someone's pursuit to do more than they thought they could. It really is the gift that keeps on giving.

RANDOM ACTS OF KINDNESS

Sometimes the smallest acts create the biggest ripples. A simple gesture, such as buying coffee for the person behind you in line, holding the door for someone with full hands, or giving up your seat on a train, can set off a chain reaction of goodwill. Acts of kindness can inspire recipients to pay it forward. What starts as one small act can multiply, becoming a wave of compassion across a community.

I experienced this firsthand at the Sydney airport. I was preparing to fly to Singapore for the second marathon of my six-marathon, six-continent, six-day challenge. A nearby family, a mom, son, and daughter, struck up a conversation with me while we waited to board. We ended up talking for over an hour about logistics, mental preparation, the physical toll, and the insanity of the challenge ahead. When it was time to go, we exchanged smiles and goodbyes, and I walked off toward the gate.

As I stood in line to board, coach ticket in hand, I was startled to see the young girl from the family walking toward me. They were headed to Singapore too. She looked at me, eyes wide with concern, and said, "I don't think you should fly coach. Not with what you're about to do. I am worried about you." Then, to my absolute astonishment, she offered me her business class seat, insisting she would take coach instead. I was floored. A complete stranger offering up her comfort, her seat, to someone she'd only just met. Her generosity stunned me.

I thanked her deeply but gently declined. My plan was to fly coach; it was part of the challenge. But that moment stuck with me. Her selfless gesture wasn't just kind; it was unforgettable. It was a ripple in motion, a reminder that goodness doesn't have to be grand to be powerful. Kindness, especially from strangers, can create waves that echo far beyond the moment.

A MENTOR'S RIPPLE

Early in my career, I didn't even know what a mentor was. My boss at the time was someone who gave instructions, evaluated performance, and left it at that. It wasn't until I met Alan that I understood the difference between a boss and a mentor.

Alan believed in me more than I believed in myself. He assigned me to projects that were beyond my experience, but he never let me fail. If I stumbled, he would sit with me, show me what I had missed, and guide me toward a better solution. He conducted his team like an orchestra, pushing each of us, especially me, to improve. His mentorship, encouragement, and guidance set me on a path of both personal and professional growth, giving me a deep and personal understanding of the impact a true mentor can have on someone's career. Years later, I've had the privilege of mentoring others, paying forward the same wisdom, support, and belief in the individual that Alan gave to me. And the ripple effect continues, with each person I've mentored going on to inspire and guide others on their own transformation.

WHY THIS MATTERS MORE THAN EVER

In a world that often feels divided and chaotic, the ripple effect reminds us of our interconnectedness. Living intentionally and creating positive ripples isn't about grand gestures; it's about consistently showing up, making mindful choices, and recognizing that we have the power to make a difference. The ripple effect shows us that living intentionally is never in vain. Even when we don't see the immediate results, our actions plant seeds of change that can grow and flourish in ways we never expected. By embracing this responsibility, we not only elevate our own lives but also inspire others to do the same.

I remember one unexpected moment at the Mandalay Bay Resort and Casino in Las Vegas. The escalator stretched long and steep, carrying convention-goers effortlessly to the second floor. It was designed for ease, for passivity. A place to stand still and let the machine do the work. But as I approached, I saw it as something different, an opportunity. Without hesitation, I stepped onto the moving stairs and began to walk up. Not because I was in a rush, but because movement, to me, is always better than standing still. Halfway up, I came upon a woman standing quietly. As I approached, I said, "Excuse me," and she shifted slightly, letting me pass without much thought. I continued, my focus already moving forward toward the exhibit floor and whatever was next. Just as I reached the entrance, I felt someone step up beside me. I turned, surprised to see the woman from the escalator. She looked at me with an intensity that told me something had shifted in her.

"Thank you for inspiring me today," she said. I hesitated, unsure of what she meant.

"Excuse me?" I asked.

She smiled, shaking her head slightly as if still processing her own realization. "You passed me on the escalator, and in that moment, it hit me, why am I just standing here? Why am I passive in my own life? I felt lost, but watching you walk by made me realize that I don't have to just stand still. I can move. I can act. Your simple act woke me up to the fact that change starts with something as small as deciding to walk up an escalator. And if I can do that, what else am I capable of? I really want to thank you for that inspiration."

I stood there for a moment, absorbing the weight of what she had just said. I hadn't set out to inspire anyone that morning. I hadn't given a speech, written a manifesto, or intentionally tried to spark an awakening in a stranger. I had simply chosen action over inaction. And yet, that small, almost insignificant choice created a ripple effect that had already touched someone else's life in a way I never could have anticipated. It was a reminder of something we often forget: our actions, no matter how small, are noticed. They create impact. They set off ripples that expand far beyond what we can see.

We often think of influence in grand terms—powerful speeches, bestselling books, acts of heroism. But true influence often starts in these kinds of somewhat innocuous moments. A kind word, a courageous choice, a quiet demonstration of persistence or discipline. They are the actions that shape the world in ways we may never fully understand. When we live intentionally, when we embody the values that we believe in, we unconsciously invite others to do the same. We become walking invitations to change. And that change doesn't have to be drastic. Sometimes, it starts with something as simple as walking up an escalator.

Think of the people who have unknowingly inspired you. The friend who started running, and, in doing so, made you believe you could run too. The colleague who took a leap into a new career, making you question whether you were settling in your own. The stranger whose kindness restored your faith in humanity, nudging you to be just a little more compassionate yourself. Every action we take has the potential to be a catalyst. Whether we realize it or not, we are constantly sending ripples into the world. And the beautiful thing about ripples is that they don't just stop; they build. They spread. They create waves of change that move through people, through communities, through cultures, and through generations.

BECOMING THE PEBBLE

The story of the escalator is just one example of how the smallest choices can carry immense power. So, what does it look like to live a life that creates positive ripples?

Live with Intentional Influence

- Model the behavior you wish to see. Your example is one of the most powerful forms of influence, whether it's courage, discipline, kindness, or resilience.

- Recognize that you are always being watched. Not in a pressure-filled way, but in the quiet way that your presence matters. Your energy, your words, your attitude, they're shaping the people around you in ways you may never fully realize.

Where Ripples Show Up

- In your family: the values we live, not just talk about, are absorbed by those closest to us.

- At work: one person's commitment, positivity, or work ethic can shift the culture of an entire team.

- In your community: small acts of service, kindness, and advocacy can inspire movements that stretch far beyond your reach.

Practical Steps to Maximize Your Ripple Effect

- Be intentional with your actions. Every choice has a consequence. Make it count.

- Share your story. Your journey, challenges included, has the power to unlock possibility in someone else.

- Practice small kindnesses. A smile, a kind word, a thank you. The smallest gestures often make the biggest waves.

- Mentor and guide. Be the person you once needed. Your experience can help someone else find their way.

- Lead by example. Actions speak louder than advice. Show up consistently with integrity.

WHAT RIPPLES ARE YOU CREATING?

Before you close this chapter, pause for a moment. Ask yourself:

1. What is one small, intentional act you've done recently that could be creating ripples, even if you don't see the impact yet?

2. Who in your life inspired you just by how they lived? How can you embody that same quiet power for someone else?

3. If you could drop one "stone" into the world today, an act of purpose, kindness, or courage, what would it be?

4. Where are you underestimating your own influence? What would happen if you owned your impact fully?

As you move through your own life, remember this: every small act matters. Every decision has weight. Every moment holds potential. You don't need a spotlight to make a difference. You just need to live intentionally. Because the ripples you create might just change someone's world.

We are the pebble.

The ripple effect is real.

And the world is better for it.

CHAPTER 11

BUILDING OUR PERSONAL HEALTH PLATFORM

Well-Being

Well-being is not just a goal; it's a declaration. A decision to live fully, with presence and purpose. It's not about chasing comfort or temporary highs; it's about aligning the body, mind, and spirit in a way that anchors us, even when life spins sideways. It is a daily act of devotion. It's the food we choose, the sleep we protect, the movement we commit to. It's the clarity we cultivate in our minds, the resilience we build in our emotions, and the connection we nurture in our relationships. It's the foundation from which everything else flows. In a world shouting at us to hustle, grind, and conform, well-being is a quiet rebellion. It's the choice to live our way, with rhythm, with boundaries, with depth. Longevity isn't just about living longer; it's about living better, more intentionally, with the strength and clarity to show up for what matters

most. Because well-being isn't a luxury. It's the platform
for our most intentional life.

A NEW WAY TO HEALTH

In an era of limitless possibilities, it is astonishing how many of
us still struggle to prioritize our health. Pursuing healthy living
is marked by a wide range of obstacles that often test our resolve
and dedication. Despite advancements in medicine, technology, and
wellness science, our personal well-being remains tethered to daily
choices that either enhance or erode our health span. It's a day-to-
day battle where temptations clash with intentions, and where time
becomes the enemy in the quest for balanced nutrition, regular exercise, and mental well-being. Amidst the fast-paced rhythms of modern life, the obstacles blocking our path to healthy living emerge in
various guises, from the allure of convenience in processed foods to
the struggle to carve out moments for self-care amidst demanding
schedules. Emotional hurdles, societal pressures, and the constant
influx of conflicting information further complicate this process. The
traditional healthcare system isn't helping much either. It's great at
fixing us when we break down, but terrible at keeping us running
smoothly in the first place.

Health needs to be redefined. It's not just about living longer, it's
about living better, longer. It's about thriving, not merely surviving.
I rarely suggest that we work on the urgent, as it is often in conflict
with the important. However, given the health trajectory we are col-
lectively on, the topic of better health is "urgent," and we need to
work on it now. We need to explore how intentional living becomes

the foundation for building our personal health platform. That is a proactive approach to well-being grounded in five essential pillars: Exercise, Nutrition, Sleep, Mindset, and Community.

Living intentionally means recognizing that our daily choices shape our well-being. Health isn't just luck or genetics; it's the result of how we live, move, eat, and rest. The real question isn't *if* we'll age, but *how.* How do you want to feel in ten, twenty, or thirty years? Are you building a life of vitality, or simply reacting when something breaks down? Sadly, many of us treat our bodies like rental cars; we drive them like we don't own them, ignore the warning lights, and hope nothing breaks down before we hand over the keys. But our bodies aren't rentals. We don't get a new one when the one we have wears out. Still, we act like there's always a backup, like the consequences won't catch up to us. And if we think the healthcare system will rescue us from poor personal maintenance, we need to realize our healthcare system isn't really about health at all. It's a sick-care system, designed to patch us up only after something goes wrong. It's like calling a mechanic after the engine has seized when it's too late to prevent the damage and you're only able to deal with the fallout. It barely works for a disposable machine, and it certainly doesn't work for the only body we've got. If we want to perform like high-performance machines, we need to treat ourselves that way, starting now.

What if we approached our health the way Formula 1 teams approach their cars? Precision. Attention. Optimization. Your body is capable of incredible things—healing, adapting, performing—but it needs more than casual upkeep. It needs a mindset of intention. Every decision we make—what we eat, how we move, and when we rest—is all a down payment on our future health. These aren't just habits; they're investments. Think about an F1 car sitting in a garage.

Essentially, it is just a very expensive paperweight. All that potential power means nothing without the right driver, the right fuel, and the right maintenance schedule. Your body works the same way. You can have the best genes in the world, but without proper care and attention, you're not going to perform at your peak. The good news? You don't need a pit crew of specialists to start treating your body like the high-performance machine it is. You just need to shift your mindset from reactive to proactive, from passenger to driver. This isn't about following some complicated regime or depriving yourself. It's about making conscious choices that align with your long-term goals. You just need to reclaim the driver's seat. Living intentionally isn't about deprivation or complexity; it's about clarity. Conscious choices that align with the life you want to live tomorrow, made today.

Want to ski at seventy? Launch a new passion project in your eighties? These aren't pipe dreams. They're outcomes that emerge from daily intention. When you stop waiting for health to "happen" to you and start shaping it yourself, everything changes. You take that F1 car out of the garage, and once you're in motion, your body begins to respond. And unlike a machine, your body actually improves with use. It gets stronger. Smarter. More resilient. That's the magic of living intentionally.

THE FIVE PILLARS OF HEALTHY LIVING

For all the biology and chemistry that are the foundation of our system, living healthy is not that complicated. We don't need an advanced degree or deep knowledge to find a path to healthy living. It starts with five essential pillars that create a personal health platform for all of us: Exercise, Nutrition, Sleep, Mindset, and Community. These pillars are interconnected, and when they work in harmony, they create a foundation for long-term vitality and well-being. Science is now confirming what we've always intuitively known: exercise is directly linked to both lifespan (how long we live) and health span (how well we live). To build a strong foundation for longevity, we need to focus on key components of health: strong mitochondria, balanced hormones, and optimal brain function (defined below). When these systems are aligned, we create a high-performance platform, our version of an F1 car, primed for peak performance and long-term health.

EXERCISE – PILLAR ONE

Pillar one is exercise. But not in the way it's often marketed. Exercise isn't about aesthetics or chasing a number on the scale; it's about *functionality* and *longevity*. Regular movement improves cardiovascular health, strengthens muscles and bones, boosts mental clarity, and elevates mood through endorphins. It regulates hormones, supports metabolic health, and dramatically lowers the risk of chronic disease.

The evidence is undeniable: exercise makes us healthier, stronger, and more resilient. And yet, we often treat it as optional. The truth is, we all have the time—we just need to give it priority. There are twenty-four hours in a day. Can we carve out just one of them to move our bodies with intention? That hour isn't a sacrifice; it's an investment. Just like we save money for our financial future, we must invest in our health to secure our future strength. Our ancestors moved constantly, walking long distances, lifting, and climbing, adapting to the world around them. Our bodies were designed for motion, not stillness. When we stop moving, we disrupt our biology and invite dysfunction. In a world built for comfort and convenience, movement no longer happens by default. We must choose it. And when we do, we reconnect with our natural state of energy, vitality, and resilience.

> Our bodies were designed for motion, not
> stillness. When we stop moving, we disrupt
> our biology and invite dysfunction. In a world
> built for comfort and convenience, movement
> no longer happens by default. We must choose
> it. And when we do, we reconnect with our
> natural state of energy, vitality, and resilience.

THE POWER OF EXERCISE

We often think of exercise in terms of what we can see: stronger muscles, better posture, improved energy. But some of its most profound effects are happening where we *can't* see, such as inside our cells, our brain, and our hormonal systems. Movement doesn't just make us feel better; it fundamentally *upgrades* how our bodies and minds function. Let's break down three invisible but essential systems that exercise supports:

Mitochondrial Health—The Cellular Engine of Longevity

Our mitochondria, often called the "powerhouses" of our cells, are responsible for producing the energy that fuels everything we do. As we age, mitochondrial function naturally declines, leading to fatigue, slower recovery, and decreased performance. However, exercise slows this decline by stimulating mitochondrial biogenesis, which increases both the number and efficiency of these cellular engines. The result?

More energy, better endurance, and greater metabolic health.[1] Think of it like tuning up a high-performance race car. You're keeping your system efficient, powerful, and built to last.

Brain Health—Movement is Mental Fuel

Exercise boosts blood flow to the brain, delivering oxygen and nutrients while triggering the release of brain-derived neurotrophic factor (BDNF), a protein that protects and repairs brain cells. BDNF functions like a software update for your brain, keeping your memory sharp, focus high, and cognition resilient against aging.[2] Regular movement also reduces the risk of cognitive decline and neurodegenerative diseases like Alzheimer's. When we move our bodies, we upgrade our brain, which enhances clarity, creativity, and decision-making.[3]

Hormonal Balance—The Body's Command System

Hormones act as the body's messaging network, directing everything from metabolism and mood to stress response. Exercise regulates insulin sensitivity, balances cortisol (our stress hormone), and boosts endorphins (our feel-good neurotransmitters). The result is improved stress resilience, mental clarity, and mood stability. Movement acts as a master reset, optimizing our internal signals and preventing the disruptions that lead to fatigue, anxiety, and burnout.[4] When we move with purpose, we do more than build strength; we activate the deep systems that keep us healthy, sharp, and emotionally grounded. It's not just fitness. It's a full-body upgrade.

THE JOY FACTOR: FIND WHAT MOVES YOU

People often see exercise as a chore, something to check off a list, a necessary but tedious task. But what if we reframed it entirely?

Movement isn't just about fitness; it's about energy, vitality, and joy. I have worked for the past twenty-five years to build a system of accountability for exercise. What started as a spreadsheet became a way of life, my C³, and was the catalyst that developed in such a way that exercise became my fourth daily habit. I eat, sleep, brush my teeth, and then exercise (my fifth habit is writing, which will be discussed later). I would sooner not brush my teeth than not exercise. What I have learned is that movement fuels my mind as much as my body. Movement to me feels like the first sip of a perfectly brewed cup of coffee. Invigorating, awakening, and deeply satisfying. It's about physical health, clarity, presence, and feeling truly alive. The more I embraced movement, the more I realized that exercise isn't something I *have* to do; it's something I *get* to do.

FUTURE-READY HEALTH: YOUR EIGHTY-YEAR-OLD SELF IS COUNTING ON YOU

The way we move today determines the body we'll live in tomorrow. Just as we invest financially for the future, we must invest physically in our longevity. The goal isn't just to live long; it's to live well. While I have a long way to go until I am eighty, I believe that I am investing in that future self. I know that the more I do, the stronger I become. It might not be at the same pace as when I was twenty, but I can hold my own and take on big challenges. I love testing myself to see how long I can hang from a pull-up bar, or how far from the grocery store I can park and carry two five-gallon jugs of water (forty pounds each). There is so much more I can do, and I look forward to doing more, not less, in the years to come. Because when I reach my magical eighty-year-old self, I will be ready for whatever life throws at me. Imagine your eighty-year-old self thanking you for the choices you made today, the strength to lift groceries, the mobility to travel, and the endurance to chase after grandkids.

Dr. Peter Attia, on his podcast *The Peter Attia Drive*, often refers to the idea of training for the "Centenarian Decathlon," the idea that we should prepare today for the physical challenges we will face in our later years.[5] This concept isn't about athletic competition; it's about ensuring that we retain the ability to carry a suitcase overhead, get up off the floor without assistance, and maintain strength and balance to prevent falls. Training for longevity means building the strength and mobility necessary to continue doing the things we love. Aging well isn't about avoiding aging; it's about maintaining vitality and function.

As Attia puts it in *Outlive: The Science and Art of Longevity*, "Exercise is by far the most potent longevity 'drug.'"[6] In other words, movement is our daily investment in future independence. Think of it like a long-term savings account; each walk, lift, stretch, or jog is a deposit toward strength, vitality, and resilience in our later years. The key is consistency. It's not about extreme workouts but about making movement a natural and regular part of our lives. Over time, our bodies adapt, becoming stronger and more resilient, allowing us to maintain our independence and functionality as we age. Ultimately, our daily movement becomes the health version of compound interest; it builds quietly, but powerfully, over time.

It's easy to understand that we can't wait thirty years to start saving for retirement, and the same applies to our health. We can't wait until problems arise to start moving. It's even "fun" (for me) to think about investing in mobility, strength, and cardiovascular health today, because the return is freedom. Freedom to move tomorrow, and the day after that, and well into the future.

THE POWER OF SMALL, CONSISTENT ACTIONS

- Address common barriers like time constraints: micro-movements add up.

- Movement stacks: short bursts of activity (five to ten minutes) throughout the day can have a significant impact.

- Incorporate movement into daily life: walk while on calls, take the stairs, and stretch in between meetings.

NUTRITION—PILLAR TWO

We are living in the most abundant food era in human history, and paradoxically, one of the sickest. At no point have we had this much access to food, convenience, and comfort. And yet, our collective health is deteriorating at a staggering rate. CDC data from 2023 confirms that over 70 percent of US Adults are overweight and over 40 percent are considered obese.[7] Ultra-processed foods (UPFs) now make up 60–70 percent of the US food supply, depending on the study. We've shifted from eating whole, natural foods to a diet dominated by packaged, chemically altered products. The problem isn't just that UPFs lack nutrients; they actively disrupt our metabolic health. They cause insulin resistance, chronic inflammation, and hormonal imbalances, setting the stage for obesity, diabetes, and cardiovascular disease. Our bodies evolved to process real food, not synthetic additives and artificial flavors. When we consume these engineered products, we confuse our body's natural regulatory systems, leading to metabolic dysfunction and long-term health issues.[8]

This isn't just a health crisis; it's a wake-up call. For many of us, it's personal. Mine came about twenty years ago, when I started noticing that my energy wasn't where I wanted it to be. My digestion felt off. I was performing, yes, but not thriving. So, I made a shift, slowly, intentionally, away from meat and toward a plant-based lifestyle. It wasn't a crash diet but a gradual evolution. At first, it was about health: I had more energy, better digestion, and a clearer mind. But over time, it became about something deeper, about protecting animals, and living more in alignment with my values. I embraced whole foods, vegetables, nuts, and fruits, and let go of most highly processed options. And to my surprise, I didn't miss the old way of eating. I actually had fun with the shift. Cooking became a creative process, and my body responded. I felt lighter, stronger, and more alive. Monica Reinagel, licensed nutritionist and host of the *Nutrition Diva* podcast, often reminds us that every bite is an opportunity to either nourish our body or detract from our health. Her practical advice encourages us to choose foods that support long-term well-being.[9]

That's what intentional health looks like. It's not punishment. It's not a rigid program. It's a path back to yourself. The reality is that the modern world makes this hard. We've engineered food to be ultra-palatable: more sugar, more salt, more fat. The kind of food that hijacks our natural hunger and fullness cues. The kind that creates a craving loop. A dopamine rush, a crash, and then repeat. Add to that a lifestyle that encourages us to sit more, move less, and outsource effort wherever possible, and you've got the perfect storm for weight gain, chronic disease, energy depletion, and steadily decreasing lifespans.

We consume more calories than we need—over 3,500 calories per day per adult in the US, on average—and we move far less than our bodies are designed to.[10] According to the EPA, when we combine our time spent indoors and in cars, we now spend more than 90 percent of our time inside.[11] Think about that: humans, who evolved in the elements, now spend nearly every waking moment surrounded by walls and screens. But here's the good news: we are not powerless. Even in a system that profits from our cravings and comfort, we still have the ability to choose. Yes, it can feel nearly impossible to lose weight on the Standard American Diet—due to the calorie density of processed foods and animal protein, it's almost a mathematical impossibility. However, my own experience, along with new data from experts like Dr. Peter Attia, offers hope, guidance, and science-backed methods for reclaiming our health. I believe I'm living proof. I've maintained the same lean, fit body weight for the past ten years, a standard that used to be typical for American men in the 1960s, before hyper-processed foods became the norm. While some may call that luck, it's not. It's the result of daily intentionality. This commitment to fueling my body with purpose and moving with intention has given me the vitality to live fully, train hard, and tackle whatever challenge comes next. You don't need perfection, but you do need a plan, and it starts with the belief that a better way is not only possible; it's entirely within reach.

Intentionality with health starts with awareness. It means noticing the patterns that no longer serve us and interrupting them. It means asking not "What do I *feel* like eating right now?" but "What will make me feel good *after* I eat it?" It means designing an environment where the easy choice is also the right one. There's a phrase one of my health advocate colleagues reminds me of all the time: "If it's in your house, it's in your mouth." Let's be honest, it's not about willpower; it's about the environment you build around yourself. For me, when I started removing processed foods from my routine, I noticed something subtle but powerful: my cravings began to change. The things I used to want, chips, sweets, and fried foods, started to lose their grip. And the things my body needed, greens, fiber, and hydration, started to become more appealing. It was like my palate reset itself. I started craving vitality instead of stimulation.

You don't have to overhaul your entire diet overnight. You just need to make one better choice. And then another. That's how we create real, lasting change. That's how we live intentionally. Yes, it's tempting to chase the quick fix. The 30-day detox. The miracle supplement. The all-in diet with the before-and-after photos. But real change comes from daily decisions, not dramatic ones. From progress, not perfection. And no, you can't outwork a bad diet. Even the most rigorous fitness routine can't overcome the impact of consistent poor nutrition. You can run marathons, lift weights, and do triathlons. But if your body is constantly inflamed, undernourished, and overstimulated by processed foods, your performance will suffer. Your energy will dip. Your recovery will lag. Eventually, something gives.

The path forward isn't about chasing the next trend. It's about coming home to simplicity. To food that grows in the ground. To movement that feels joyful. To rest that restores. Health is not about achieving perfection. It's about creating alignment between your values and your habits. Do I still enjoy good food? Absolutely. But now I define "good" differently. Good means nourishing, energizing, and life-giving. It means food that supports the kind of life I want to live, a life of endurance, purpose, and presence. You don't need to be plant-based to live intentionally, but you *do* need to be aware. To notice what you eat. To observe how it makes you feel. To recognize when you're eating from habit, stress, or boredom. And to remind yourself with compassion that you are in charge.

EATING INTENTIONALLY ON THE ROAD

Living intentionally with food isn't just about what you do at home; it's about how you show up when life gets chaotic. And for me, that includes travel. I'm on the road a lot, which means airports, hotels, unfamiliar cities, and tight schedules. Over the past twenty-five years, I have flown five million miles and stayed in hotels over six thousand nights. These environments are not designed for optimal health. But that's never been an excuse for me to throw intentionality out the window. In fact, it's where it matters most. One of the things I've learned over the years is this: if you want to stay on track, you must be intentional. I don't leave my nutrition to chance. I bring my own fuel, always.

My go-to travel kit includes items like almonds and walnuts, bran cereal, and high-quality protein powder. If I need a packaged food, it must have fewer than seven ingredients. Simple, clean, and portable. I know how these foods make me feel. I know they provide sustained energy without the crash. Plus, they keep me grounded when everything else around me is in motion. Over time, I've added a few more staples: a reusable water bottle I fill after security, packets of nut butter, high-quality energy bars, and even bags of grapes or sliced apples I pack from home. Sometimes, I'll bring single-serve oats, a shaker bottle for mixing protein, or a small container of chia seeds to enhance any meal. I've learned that it's worth bringing what fuels me, even if it means planning ahead.

There's something powerful about choosing intentionality—even in an airport terminal surrounded by fast food and sugary snacks. It's not about being rigid; it's about being aligned. You can walk past the convenience store, knowing you're already prepared. You can say no to the mystery buffet and yes to your health. You can feel good in your body, no matter where you are in the world. When we live this way, our environment no longer dictates our choices. We become the architects of our own well-being, wherever we go.

PERSONALIZED NUTRITION: FINDING WHAT WORKS FOR YOU

While there's no single "perfect diet," certain core principles apply to nearly everyone. The building blocks are the three macronutrients that we all need every day and in good proportion:

- **Protein:** Essential for muscle maintenance, satiety, and metabolic function.

- **Healthy Fats:** Support brain health, hormone balance, and sustained energy.

- **Fiber-Rich Carbohydrates:** Our metabolic energy source to support our performance needs while regulating blood sugar and supporting gut health.

Beyond the basics, discovering your personal optimal diet requires experimentation and self-awareness. Some people thrive on a low-carb diet, while others need more carbs to fuel performance. The key is to listen to your body, track how you feel after meals, and adjust accordingly. Your ideal nutrition plan should support both energy and mental clarity.

Most of my friends know I have a lot of discipline. They often shake their heads at how I can stick to the same routine day after day. But if I have a goal, and that goal requires consistency, I don't get bored, I get focused. I used that mindset to take control of my nutrition. I found what worked for my body and stuck with it. For years, I ate essentially the same three meals every day. During my most intense Ironman training, lunch was always the same: a peanut butter sandwich, a side of broccoli, and a protein bar. Not for a week. Not for a season. For five straight years. And I loved it. That lunch became an anchor, a daily reminder of the path I was on and the discipline that fueled it. A moment of predictability and nourishment in an otherwise intense training schedule. It wasn't flashy, but it worked, and it made a real difference in my performance. At its core, nutrition is about shifting from mindless consumption to purposeful nourishment. When we eat with awareness, recognizing hunger and satiety cues, choosing foods that serve us, and honoring our body's signals, we create a deeper connection between food and function. Every meal becomes an opportunity: to fuel performance, support longevity, and align our choices with our goals. The aim isn't perfection; it's alignment. Eating with intention builds the foundation for long-term health, resilience, and vitality.

FOOD AS FUEL FOR A HIGH-PERFORMANCE LIFE

In the end, nutrition is not about willpower or fads; it's about alignment. Just like the other pillars of intentional living, eating well is an act of self-respect. It's a daily choice to give your body the support it needs to show up fully for life's demands and dreams. Food becomes more than just fuel; it becomes part of your identity. The goal is never rigid perfection, but deep attunement. What nourishes you physically should also nourish you mentally and emotionally. When you approach each meal as a moment of intention, a vote for your future self, you begin to eat not just to satisfy hunger, but to optimize your energy, elevate your mood, and extend your vitality.

What I've come to realize is this: the most powerful diet is the one you don't have to think about. It's the one that supports your goals, aligns with your values, and feels effortless because it's been tested and trusted over time. Like a rhythm you can dance to. Nutrition, then, becomes not a restriction, but a form of freedom. So, ask yourself: "What do I want my nutrition to say about how I live?" And then eat in a way that answers that question with clarity and conviction.

SLEEP–PILLAR THREE

Of all the tools available to us in the pursuit of health and longevity, sleep might be the most underestimated, and the most powerful. We often treat it as an afterthought, a luxury we can sacrifice in the name of productivity. But sleep is not a break from progress. It *is* the progress. It's not just rest; it's repair, recalibration, and renewal. Sleep is where the body performs its deepest work: regulating hormones, healing tissues, consolidating memories, and sharpening focus. And still, over fifty million Americans struggle to get enough of it. The irony is striking. While we chase more time by cutting sleep short, we're diminishing the *quality* of the time we have.

We now know that sleep is a dynamic and deeply active process. It cycles through multiple stages, light sleep, deep sleep, and REM, each playing a distinct and essential role. Light sleep prepares the brain for restoration and consolidates motor skills. Deep sleep handles the heavy lifting: physical repair, immune function, and the release of growth hormone. REM sleep, often associated with dreaming, supports emotional processing, creativity, and memory formation. When this cycle is disrupted—whether by late-night screen time, stress, poor habits, drugs, alcohol, or inconsistency—we lose more than rest; we lose access to our body's natural systems for growth, repair, and performance.

For those of us who train our bodies, whether for a race, an adventure, or the demands of daily life, sleep becomes our most important recovery tool. During deep sleep, the body rebuilds muscle tissue, restores energy reserves, and enhances immune resilience. REM sleep improves motor learning, reaction time, and coordination. Without enough of either, performance begins to falter. Recovery slows. The risk of injury increases. Focus and decision-making suffer. But this isn't just about sports. We are all athletes in some capacity, pushing toward goals, adapting to pressure, trying to show up with strength. And for all of us, the equation holds: training hard is meaningless if we don't recover deeply.

THE LINK BETWEEN SLEEP AND LONGEVITY

Even more compelling is the growing evidence linking sleep to long-term health and longevity. Researchers now recognize that high-quality, consistent sleep reduces the risk of chronic disease, from heart conditions and Alzheimer's to cancer and metabolic disorders. Deep sleep supports cellular repair and reduces inflammation, both essential to aging well. Poor sleep, on the other hand, accelerates biological aging by disrupting hormone balance, increasing oxidative stress, and impairing brain function. Individuals who consistently sleep fewer than six hours per night have a higher risk of mortality compared to those who prioritize restorative sleep. Dr. Matthew Walker, author of *Why We Sleep*, states: "Sleep is the single most effective thing we can do to reset our brain and body health each day."[12]

MASTERING SLEEP FOR LONGEVITY
AND PEAK PERFORMANCE

So, how do we reclaim the power of sleep? We must treat it as a non-negotiable part of intentional living:

- **Keep a Consistent Sleep Schedule:** Going to bed and waking up at the same time daily regulates circadian rhythm.

- **Control Light Exposure:** Morning sunlight exposure and avoiding blue light at night optimizes melatonin production.

- **Create a Sleep Sanctuary:** A cool, dark, quiet room (60–67 degrees Farenheit) enhances deep sleep.

- **Manage Stress Before Bed:** Breathwork, meditation, or journaling reduce cortisol, making sleep restorative instead of restless.

- **Avoid Late-Night Eating and Alcohol:** Both disrupt deep sleep and impair recovery.

- **Optimize Nutrition and Supplements:** Magnesium, glycine, and theanine support deeper sleep cycles.

- **Caffeine Cutoff Time:** No caffeine eight hours before bed to avoid sleep fragmentation.

- **Cold Exposure:** A short cold shower or cool bedroom enhances deep sleep.

Neuroscientist Dr. Andrew Huberman, host of the *Huberman Lab* podcast, often emphasizes that sleep is the foundation of mental and physical performance. He describes it as one of the most powerful and most overlooked tools we have for improving every aspect of our health.[13]

He's right. When we treat sleep with the same discipline and reverence that we bring to our nutrition or our training, we unlock an entirely new level of vitality and performance. Sleep is not something we do once the day is over. It's something that *makes the day possible.* And when we protect it, when we prioritize it as essential, we don't just wake up feeling better. We lead better, think more clearly, and move through life more intentionally. Sleep is the foundation beneath it all. It is how we restore our strength, reinforce our growth, and extend our health span.

MINDSET—PILLAR FOUR

Our mindset shapes our reality. A positive, growth-oriented mindset can profoundly impact our health. Stress, anxiety, and negative thought patterns can erode our well-being, while a mindset focused on possibility and resilience can enhance it. Research in neuroplasticity shows that our brain is constantly adapting based on our thoughts and experiences. A growth mindset, coined by psychologist Carol Dweck, fosters resilience and adaptability, while a fixed mindset limits progress.[14] Intentional living isn't about thinking in absolutes or avoiding hardship; it's about shifting our response to it.

- Reframing failure as feedback allows us to turn obstacles into learning opportunities.

- Cognitive behavioral therapy (CBT) teaches us how to challenge limiting beliefs and replace them with empowering narratives.

- Mental resilience is a muscle. The more we practice adapting to adversity, the stronger we become.

MINDSET AND PHYSICAL HEALTH: THE MIND-BODY CONNECTION

The deeper we go and the more we think about it, the more we realize that the mind and body are an integrated system. They are not separate. Our thoughts directly impact hormone regulation, immune resilience, and recovery from illness. The placebo effect demonstrates how belief alone can influence healing. Conversely, we have all felt the effects of chronic stress and negative thinking when we get sick faster and recover more slowly.

DAILY MINDSET PRACTICES FOR INTENTIONAL LIVING

- **Mental Priming:** Starting the day with an intentional focus (affirmations, visualization). My good friend, Joe D., has the following quote as his home screen: "My purpose is to raise my level of consciousness through awareness, with the intention of serving humanity and making the world a more loving place." It is a great example of the power of words and how he must feel every time he looks at his phone.

- **Embracing Discomfort:** In Chapter 3, we made the case that discomfort is an integral part of our lives and that we need to push ourselves to view discomfort as a catalyst for growth. Make discomfort appealing and great things happen.

- **Resilience Training:** We are learning that there are a lot of ways that we can easily access techniques that build mental toughness through controlled adversity. Cold exposure has gained attention as a powerful method, not just for its physical benefits, but also for its mental resilience training. Exposure to cold triggers the body's stress response in a controlled way, helping individuals adapt to discomfort, improve emotional regulation, and strengthen their ability to handle real-world challenges. Other forms of controlled adversity include:

  » **Fasting:** Strengthening discipline and metabolic flexibility by withholding food for set periods.

  » **Endurance Training:** Activities like long-distance running or high-intensity training that push mental and physical limits.

Each of these methods rewires our brain to develop greater perseverance, discipline, and grit, helping us build the resilience needed for intentional living.

Mindset is also about self-compassion. It's recognizing that we are human, that setbacks happen, and that growth is a progressive evolution over time. In his book, *The Plantpower Way*, Rich Roll writes, "Rather than flog yourself over a slip, embrace it as simply an integral part of the process of change."[15] By being kind to ourselves, we create space for sustained, intentional growth.

Prioritizing our mindset isn't about ignoring difficulties; it's about deciding how we engage with them. Challenges will always exist, but the way we frame them determines whether they limit us or propel us forward. When we intentionally shape our thoughts, we don't just shift our perspective; we unlock the potential for transformation in every area of our lives. Our mindset isn't just a concept; it's the operating system that shapes our reality. When we take true ownership of our thoughts, we gain the power to rewrite our story, turning obstacles into opportunities and setbacks into stepping stones.

COMMUNITY–PILLAR FIVE

Humans are social creatures, and our health is deeply influenced by our relationships. Loneliness and isolation have been linked to various health issues, including depression, anxiety, and even a shorter lifespan. Intentional living means nurturing meaningful connections. It's about surrounding ourselves with people who uplift and support us, and it's about contributing to our communities in meaningful ways.

A strong social network provides emotional support, reduces stress, and gives us a sense of purpose. Community can be found in family, friends, colleagues, or even online groups that share our interests and values. Dr. Robert Waldinger, director of the Harvard Study on Adult Development, found that the number one predictor of a long, healthy life isn't genetics, diet, or exercise; it's relationships.[16]

Much has been written about the Blue Zones' longevity formula, in regions where people consistently live past one hundred (Okinawa, Japan; Sardinia, Italy; Nicoya, Costa Rica; Ikaria, Greece; Loma Linda, California). The most common factors affecting their lifespan seem to be:

- Strong social networks.

- Meaningful relationships.

- Purpose (*Ikigai*). Having a reason to get up each morning.

- Daily movement.

- Plant-based diets.[17]

It seems like quite a simple formula, but it requires intention and alignment to make it happen.

HEALTH SPAN: LIVING BETTER, LONGER

The concept of health span focuses on the quality of life, not just the quantity. It's about maximizing our years of vitality and functionality, ensuring that we can continue to pursue our passions and live with purpose as we age. Dr. Peter Attia emphasizes the importance of focusing on health span to ensure that extended years are lived with quality and vitality. In his book *Outlive: The Science and Art of Longevity*, Dr. Attia advocates for a proactive approach to health, emphasizing early screening, personalized health management, and lifestyle adjustments to prevent age-related diseases.[18]

As I have discovered, health span is tied to resilience. That is the ability to bounce back from challenges and the capacity to perform daily tasks with ease. It's about being active and curious, maintaining our independence, and continuing to grow and learn throughout life. Even after a fall on a trail race, I can bounce back faster than if I had not leaned heavily into the underlying ideas behind health span. So, now I spend every day building my personal health platform, ultimately extending my health span. When we invest in practices that enhance our vitality, we get to live fully and intentionally for as long as possible.

NEW THINKING ON HEALTH: TRENDS AND POSSIBILITIES

The landscape of health and wellness is evolving rapidly. New technologies, such as wearable devices and personalized health apps, are empowering individuals to take control of their health like never before. Genetic testing, telemedicine, and advances in preventive care are opening new possibilities for proactive health management. But with these advancements comes the responsibility to use them intentionally. Technology should be a tool to enhance our health, not a distraction. It's about integrating new solutions thoughtfully into our personal health platforms. Trends such as biohacking, longevity research, and holistic wellness practices are gaining traction, offering new ways to optimize our well-being. The potential is vast, but it requires a commitment to continuous learning and adaptation.

CONNECTING INTENTIONAL LIVING WITH HEALTH

At its core, building a personal health platform is about intentional living. It's about recognizing that every choice we make matters, that our daily actions have a cumulative impact on our health span. Living intentionally means committing to the practices that enhance our well-being. It's about showing up for ourselves every day, making small, purposeful choices that add up to a life of vitality and resilience. Health is not something we achieve overnight. It's a process, a lifelong commitment to ourselves. We should be excited and thrilled that we *can* make a difference in our lives every day, and that we do not need to win some health lottery or have Olympic-level genetics. By embracing the five pillars of healthy living and staying curious about new possibilities, we will build a personal health platform that supports us through life's challenges and opportunities.

As we learn, our health is our most valuable asset. It is the foundation upon which we build our dreams, relationships, and contributions to the world. By living intentionally, we ensure that we are not just adding years to our lives, but life to our years. And in doing so, we create a life of depth, energy, and purpose, one day at a time.

CHAPTER 12

LIVING BEYOND OURSELVES

Escape Velocity

We all know that moment. Standing at the edge of something big, heart racing, knowing we're about to jump into the unknown and do more than we ever thought possible. In science, it is called escape velocity, the precise speed a rocket needs to break free from Earth's gravitational pull. In our lives, it is when we break free from the pull of complacency, fear, or self-doubt and reach the point where we are propelled toward our true potential. Much like a spacecraft needs a specific amount of speed to overcome Earth's gravity, we too must build momentum through discipline, resilience, and the courage to take risks. It requires mental and emotional strength and a willingness to go forward even in the face of adversity. Once we achieve our escape velocity, limitations fall away, and we soar. Reaching our escape velocity isn't just about overcoming obstacles; it's about setting ourselves free to live with meaning and purpose and achieve things we never thought possible: that magnificent moment when the force of our determination finally overcomes the weight of our fears. And once we're there, we discover just how far we really can go.

LIFTING OTHERS, RISING TOGETHER

It's human nature to begin life focused on ourselves, our goals, our careers, our needs, and our desires. And for a while, that's necessary. We must build our foundation, figure out who we are, and discover what we're capable of. But there comes a moment when we realize that living solely for ourselves is not enough. True fulfillment doesn't come from what we gain; it comes from what we give. To live intentionally is to live beyond ourselves. It means understanding that our actions, our choices, and our contributions ripple far beyond the boundaries of our own lives. We've all been shaped by people who chose to live this way: teachers, coaches, parents, mentors, friends, and colleagues. People who gave us time, encouragement, or belief when we needed it most. Their generosity lit a path for us. And at some point, we feel the call to do the same, to pay it forward. I feel this deeply when I coach budding entrepreneurs. I might be offering them guidance, but often, I walk away inspired. That's the beautiful paradox of giving: when we live beyond ourselves, we don't just lift others, we rise with them.

James Clear, in *Atomic Habits*, writes, "Every action you take is a vote for the type of person you wish to become."[1] That's the heart of intentional living. It's not about one defining moment; it's about a series of choices, repeated consistently, that shape who we are. And when those choices are rooted in contribution, when we show up not just for ourselves, but for others, that's when we reach our personal escape velocity. That's when we start to rise. Living intentionally isn't just about personal growth; it's about creating a life that matters. Every element we've explored so far contributes to a larger mosaic. But now we arrive at a deeper question: What kind of impact do we want to have? How do we want to shape the world around us? And ultimately, how do we want to be remembered? The answers to these questions define what it means to live beyond ourselves. When we commit to this path, we become role models, often without even realizing it. Our actions, our choices, and the way we navigate challenges are noticed. They ripple outward. Angela Duckworth, in her book *Grit*, reminds us that success stems from perseverance and passion sustained over time.[2] That same endurance is what makes a lasting impression, not just on our own path, but on the people watching us walk it.

Role models aren't only found on stages or in history books. They live in our neighborhoods, they're in our offices, and they're part of our families. They are the managers who lead with heart, the friends who show up when it matters, and the mentors who give their time without expectation. Small acts, such as mentoring a colleague, helping a neighbor, and offering encouragement, can have an outsized impact. When we choose to live beyond ourselves, we don't just change lives. We shape legacies. I've learned that living beyond ourselves starts with a simple offer, not to the universe exactly, but to the people we encounter every day. For the past ten years, I've extended an open invitation to a thirty-minute meeting to every employee at the companies where I've been CEO on any topic they choose. No agenda required. Just time with each other. It's become a way for me to connect with my team, to listen, to share, and to understand what matters most to them. And while it may seem like a small gesture, it's given me so much in return. I feel more connected, more grounded, and more in tune with the heartbeat of the organization. And honestly? I think they benefit too. At least, I hope so.

LIVING BEYOND YOURSELF: THE GIFT OF MENTORSHIP

I still remember the knot in my stomach when I first became CEO. Every decision felt weighty, every board meeting loomed large, and questions swirled in my head like leaves in an autumn storm. But I was lucky. I had someone in my corner, our chairman, who showed me what it meant to live a life that mattered. He wasn't just successful; he was significant. Sure, he'd built thriving businesses, but that wasn't what defined him. You'd find him hosting fundraisers in his historic brownstone, championing the Boston Ballet, or quietly opening doors for causes he believed in. But what amazed me most was how he made time for me.

Once a month, we'd meet in his home library. Picture this: warm wood panels, leather-bound books, and above the door, words from John Adams that still echo in my mind: "We cannot ensure success, but we can deserve it." In that room, surrounded by centuries of wisdom, he taught me about leadership, not through lectures, but through patient guidance and thoughtful questions. After half a year of these sessions, I worked up the courage to ask how I was doing. His response was just one word: "Better." Not exactly a ringing endorsement, but perfectly honest. That simple word taught me more about growth than any management book ever could.

Today, I find myself on the other side of that table, mentoring new CEOs who carry the same doubts I once did. It's funny how life comes full circle. What I've learned is that true leadership isn't just about strategy or execution. It's about lifting others as you climb. My mentor didn't just teach me how to lead a company; he showed me how to lead a life worth living.

WHY LIVING INTENTIONALLY MEANS CONTRIBUTING TO THE WORLD

Many of us move through life without ever pausing to consider the legacy we're leaving behind. We get swept up in the busyness of daily routines and forget to ask the bigger questions: "What will my impact be? How will the world be different because I was here?" Living beyond ourselves requires a shift in perspective. It means showing up with resilience, compassion, and purpose. When we embody those qualities, we create a ripple effect that reaches far beyond what we can see. Few people have demonstrated this more profoundly than Viktor Frankl in *Man's Search for Meaning,* where he reveals that discovering purpose, especially through service, can bring deep fulfillment.[3] His story is a reminder that we always have a choice to live for something greater than ourselves.

When we live with intention, we naturally inspire others to do the same. We become more aware of how our choices ripple outward, shaping our families, communities, and culture. We prioritize kindness, generosity, and service, not out of obligation, but because it feels like the most meaningful way to live. In that light, success becomes less about status or wealth, and more about contribution to our communities, our planet, and future generations. But believing in the power of intentional living isn't enough. We must embody it. Living beyond ourselves begins with a mindset shift, with daily choices, and with the courage to trust that our actions matter. For some, like Greta Thunberg, that clarity arrives early. For others, like me, it takes time. But timing is secondary. What matters is that once we awaken to our deeper purpose, we choose to give back, to lift others, and to leave the world better than we found it.

> Success becomes less about status or wealth, and
> more about contribution to our communities,
> our planet, and future generations.

When we go through life with open eyes and an open heart, we create space for extraordinary opportunities. That's exactly what happened when I was talking to Katie, one of my favorite people, about what she was up to. She mentioned that she was involved with an entrepreneurship program for formerly incarcerated people. *Wow! What an interesting idea*, I thought. The program, sponsored by Defy Ventures, provides mentorship to help people build and launch their own businesses after incarceration. Defy has been doing this work for over thirteen years, and I was immediately intrigued. I asked how I could get involved.

The first step was attending a "pitch day," where the Entrepreneurs in Training (EITs) presented their business ideas to a panel, like a kinder version of *Shark Tank*. It was nothing short of remarkable. Listening to the pitches, feeling the energy in the room, and watching the panel offer encouragement and thoughtful feedback was deeply inspiring. I left that day completely committed, knowing I wanted to get more involved.

Over the following months, my engagement with Defy Ventures deepened and eventually led to a field trip to the heart of the program: a ten-month Entrepreneurship in Training program inside a female maximum-security prison in California. From the moment we arrived, I knew this would be no ordinary day. We passed through the usual protocol—guards, fences, IDs, forms, and rules—inside a gray, cinder-block building. As we waited for clearance, the small talk among our group felt forced, like we all sensed the gravity of where we were. For a moment, my thoughts drifted: *How does a system like this become necessary? Why don't we do more to prevent it? What more can I do?* A firm "Let's go," from the lead guard jolted me back. We filed through the gates in a single file.

The hundred-yard walk to the next building felt heavy. Three layers of fencing, spirals of concertina wire, and looming towers reminded us of the reality we were entering. But the moment we stepped inside the function room, everything changed. Fifty cheering EITs greeted us, all in prison-issued uniforms, smiling and high-fiving us as we entered. The energy was electric, joyful, vibrant, and unexpected. I asked myself: *What is happening? How could there be so much positivity in a place like this?* It was surreal, the kind of emotional whiplash that leaves a lasting mark.

Each of the mentors was paired with three EITs. Our task was to listen to their business pitches, provide feedback, and vote to select finalists across multiple rounds. But this day wasn't just about business; it became something much deeper. We shared in powerful, emotionally charged conversations about empathy, vulnerability, and resilience. Many of the EITs were serving life sentences. That reality sank in as I listened to them describe their dreams—businesses they hoped to build if they were ever released. It was both heartbreaking and inspiring. Their hope, in the face of such uncertainty, was extraordinary.

Reality would interrupt us periodically. Guards entered for routine "counts," a sobering reminder of where we were. But even amid these interruptions, I wasn't there to judge. I was there to bear witness to their courage, their humanity, and their pursuit of redemption. And perhaps most surprisingly, despite having no internet access or computers, their business plans were as developed, creative, and well-researched as many I'd seen from early-stage founders "on the outside."

At the end of the day, I was asked to give the commencement speech. It was one of the hardest I've ever delivered. What could I say to people who had already faced so much? I returned to the basics—the foundation of human connection. I spoke about respect. Respect for their perseverance, for their lives, and for the idea that hope must endure, even in the hardest places. When I finished, I felt profoundly different—more grounded, more connected. That kind of transformation only happens when we allow ourselves to go to emotional depths we don't often visit.

The day continued with celebrations and applause. A winner was announced, cake and coffee were shared, and then it was time to leave. As we were saying our goodbyes, one of the women I had spoken with several times throughout the day handed me a folded piece of paper. Inside were four handwritten words: "Please never forget us." I slipped the note into my pocket and walked back through the gates, wiping away tears as we exited the facility. Those four words have stayed with me every day since.

LIVING BEYOND OURSELVES

Living beyond ourselves requires a shift in perspective. That day was a culmination of my own path of living intentionally, not just helping run the program or giving the speech, but in showing up with presence and empathy. I think about that note often. Imagine if we each received a similar note from the people we encounter in life. How would we feel? What kind of impact did we make? What impact did they have on us? Once we start asking these questions, we realize that true purpose extends far beyond our own needs. Living intentionally means showing up for others, even when it's uncomfortable, even when it's hard. By caring deeply about our community and making a meaningful difference in the lives of others, we create a legacy that matters. That's what living beyond ourselves is all about: leaving the world better than we found it.

WHAT IS LEGACY AND WHY SHOULD WE CARE?

Legacy is often associated with grand achievements or monumental contributions, but it doesn't have to be. Our legacy is the sum of the values we live by and the impact we have on others. It's about how people remember us, and the ways in which our life influences future generations. They remember us for what we did and how we gave to others. We rarely, if ever, need to remind someone of our "importance" to have a legacy that matters. Rather, legacy is earned. The question to ask is: Do people with whom we have interacted live differently because they knew us or spent time with us?

Consider the story of Fred Rogers, better known as Mister Rogers, the charismatic and empathetic host of *Mister Rogers' Neighborhood*. His legacy wasn't built on fame or fortune. It was built on kindness, empathy, and an unwavering belief in the inherent worth of every person. He made people feel seen, valued, and loved. That's a legacy that endures far beyond his lifetime. Rogers said, "The greatest gift you ever give is your honest self."[4] The way he showed up, intentionally, day after day, for decades, inspired multiple generations to build self-confidence and tap into their authentic selves. Thus, his iconic legacy was built and will transcend future generations.

Legacy matters because it reminds us that our lives extend beyond the present moment. It's easy to get swept up in the demands of daily life. But when we pause to consider the impact we wish to leave behind, we are called to live with a deeper purpose. Legacy isn't just about achievements, it's about how we make others feel, the values we embody, and the lives we quietly shape. Too often, legacy is misunderstood as something reserved for the famous or the powerful. But every one of us leaves a legacy in the lives we touch, our families, our communities, and our coworkers. It lives in the small acts of kindness, the stories we tell, and the examples we set. We can often pinpoint our specific viewpoints, preferences, and sometimes even our identity based on "how grandma did it" or "what dad would have said." Their influence lives on in the way we speak, the decisions we make, and the values we uphold. Legacy is not about being remembered by the world; it's about being remembered by the people who matter. And when we live with intention, we don't just carry their legacy forward; we become one for someone else.

Think about your local community. The teacher who mentors struggling students, the neighbor who volunteers at a food bank (like my sister, who for twenty years led the efforts at her local food pantry), the friend who is always there to lend a hand. These are the people who create lasting legacies through their everyday actions. We don't need a platform or a title to make an impact. We just need to show up, consistently, with kindness and purpose.

Every one of us leaves a legacy in the lives we
touch, our families, our communities, and our
coworkers. It lives in the small acts of kindness,
the stories we tell, and the examples we set.

Jimmy Carter, the thirty-ninth US President, is a powerful example of someone who built a legacy through service, humility, and an unwavering commitment to others. After his presidency, he could have chosen a life of comfort and prestige, cashing in on the privileges that come with having held the highest office in the land. Instead, he redefined what it means to be a former president, dedicating himself to humanitarian efforts, diplomacy, and global health initiatives. While many know of his hands-on work with Habitat for Humanity, Carter's impact extends far beyond building homes. Through The Carter Center, he spearheaded initiatives to combat diseases like Guinea-worm disease, malaria, and river blindness—illnesses that had long plagued the most impoverished corners of the world. His relentless efforts led to a near-eradication of Guinea-worm disease, proving that with determination and focused action, global health challenges could be met head-on.

Carter also played a crucial role in international peacekeeping and diplomacy. Long after leaving the White House, he remained a trusted mediator, brokering peace agreements and monitoring elections in fragile democracies. His efforts helped foster stability in countries where democracy teetered on the edge, reinforcing his belief that leadership isn't about power, but about service. He didn't seek fame or recognition; he sought impact. His legacy isn't defined solely by his time in office but by his decades of tireless service to others. He showed us that legacy is not about titles or accolades; it's about how we choose to spend our time, energy, and resources to lift others up. Carter's life is a testament to the idea that true leadership is measured not by how long you hold power, but by how much good you do with the time you have. It certainly gives us all a standard to shape the arc of our lives with meaning and grace.

CREATING A PERSONAL IMPACT PLAN

So, how do we begin to live beyond ourselves? It starts with the desire to make a difference. Can you recall a time when you did something purely for someone else, when you used your time and energy not for gain, but for good? Let those moments be the spark. They're the foundation for your personal impact plan, a roadmap for how you want to contribute to the world and leave it better than you found it.

1. Identify Your Core Values

Our core values are the foundation of a meaningful life. What do you stand for? What principles guide your decisions? These values will shape how you show up in the world and the legacy you leave behind. Take time to reflect. Are you passionate about environmental sustainability? Education? Equality? Community service? Whatever your values are, let them guide your actions.

2. Define Your Purpose

Purpose is our reason for being. It's the internal compass that points us toward contribution. Ask yourself: "What do I care about deeply? What problems move me? How can I use my strengths and resources to make a difference?" Purpose doesn't require grandeur.

It starts with meaningful acts in the spaces where you already have influence.

3. Set Impact Goals

With values and purpose as your foundation, set specific goals. They can be small or bold. From mentoring a student to launching a nonprofit. The key is to make them actionable and aligned with who you are.

4. Take Consistent Action

Impact isn't born from a single gesture. It's built through steady, intentional effort over time. Commit to small acts that reflect your values. Those efforts will compound, quietly shaping the world around you.

5. Reflect and Adjust

Living beyond yourself is not a one-time event; it's a way of being. Make space for regular reflection. Are your actions aligned with your values? Is your impact creating the change you envisioned? This reflection keeps your path true and your purpose fresh.

WHY THIS MATTERS

Living beyond ourselves shifts our focus from what we can get out of life to what we can give. It's about creating a legacy of kindness, generosity, and purpose. It's about being a force for good, one intentional act at a time. Simon Sinek, in *The Infinite Game*, reminds us that true leaders play for long-term impact, not short-term wins.[5] That kind of mindset builds a more compassionate, connected, and resilient world. It invites others to rise, too. And in the process, we uncover deeper meaning in our own lives. Sinek also shared, in a conversation on *The Diary of a CEO* podcast, "There's no greater honor than being able to serve a friend in need."[6] That single sentence captures a life of empathy, service, and purpose, a legacy to be proud of.

LEGACY BEGINS NOW

Legacy isn't just something we leave behind; it's something we live every day. It's not built in marble or etched in monuments. It's built in the moments when we show up with compassion. When we choose integrity over convenience. When we offer our time, our presence, or our belief in someone else. Living beyond ourselves doesn't require a stage or a spotlight. It requires intention and the courage to act on it. The truth is, most of us won't ever know the full extent of our impact. We won't see every life we've touched, or every ripple we've set in motion. But that doesn't make it any less real.

That's the beauty of it.

We plant seeds we may never see grow.

We light paths we may never walk.

We become the reason someone else chooses to rise.

And that is more than enough.

So live boldly.

Give generously.

Lead with heart.

**And trust that your legacy is already unfolding—
one intentional moment at a time.**

CHAPTER 13

THE ENDLESS JOURNEY

Limitless Thinking

There is no summit in a life fully lived, only ever-widening vistas. To dream, to imagine, to reach beyond the stars: this is not fantasy, but our invitation. Growth is not a destination; it is a way of being, an ongoing exploration of what is possible. Limitless thinking is the key to this beautiful gift called life. It allows us to break free from boundaries we once believed were fixed. It dares us to challenge the constraints we've imposed on ourselves, to stretch into the unknown, and to see beyond what we once thought was possible. Life is not only about going farther, but also about going deeper. Into our purpose. Into our consciousness and awareness. Into who we are. With each step forward, we shed the illusions of limitation and move closer to self-actualization. Not as a finish line, but as a way of being—awake, alive, and intentional. The only true limits are the ones we accept. When we choose otherwise, we step into a life of infinite possibility.

WHEN "I MADE IT" ISN'T THE END

There was a time when I thought success had a finish line. That if I just reached a certain level, whether in work, relationships, or personal growth, I could check the box and finally say, "I made it." First, it was my career: becoming a partner and climbing the corporate ladder, thinking that once I got there, something inside would shift. Then it was Ironman racing, chasing a spot at the Triathlon World Championship in Kona as if that accomplishment would make me whole. After that, it was business, starting companies, imagining that a big exit would be the final piece of the puzzle. I remember crossing the finish line at my first Ironman in Tempe, Arizona, with my best friend, Joe. After eleven hours and fifty-nine minutes of swimming, biking, and running, I had hit my goal: sub-twelve hours. I felt euphoric, even though I was physically wrecked and emotionally raw. I had told friends and family this would be the moment, the culmination of five years of training, twenty-hour weeks, countless prep races, and sacrifices. I was an Ironman. But the next morning, limping around the hotel room, the high began to fade. Was I going to need to do another one? Was I already thinking about what's next? That's when it hit me: there is no final, "I made it." Life doesn't work that way. There's only the next race, the next challenge, the next horizon, and the next step forward.

Intentional living isn't about arrival. It's about evolution. It's not a destination we reach and check off a list. It's a daily practice, a conscious choice to show up, reflect, and renew. It's about learning to live with purpose and presence, even when the road ahead isn't clear. It is about going deeper into our consciousness, our understanding, and our purpose. With each step, we shed the illusions of limitation and move closer to self-actualization, to a state of being that cannot be reached without deliberate intention. This is the path not just of growth, but of awakening. An unfolding toward wisdom, clarity, and the highest expression of who we are meant to be. Not to prove something. But to become something.

> Intentional living isn't about arrival. It's about evolution. It's not a destination we reach and check off a list. It's a daily practice, a conscious choice to show up, reflect, and renew. It's about learning to live with purpose and presence, even when the road ahead isn't clear.

LIFE AS THE INFINITE GAME

This shift, from achievement to becoming, is what defines the "Infinite Game." It's no longer about finishing. It's about being and continuing. Simon Sinek calls this perspective the "Infinite Game."[1] Life isn't about winning or losing; it's about continuously improving, adapting, and evolving. In an infinite game, we aren't competing against others, but against our past selves. This is the essence of intentional living. There is no ultimate arrival, no final milestone. Instead, there is only the next step forward, the next moment of awareness, the next conscious choice.

David Goggins, a former Navy SEAL and ultramarathon runner, explains it perfectly in *Can't Hurt Me*: "Most of us give up when we've only given around 40 percent of our maximum effort." Goggins argues that we are capable of far more than we realize—mentally, physically, emotionally—but we stop short because discomfort convinces us we've reached our limit. There's always more. The goal isn't to eliminate discomfort; it's to train yourself to lean into it. That's where growth happens. We are not designed to plateau. We are designed to grow.[2] I have long loved Joseph Campbell's way of describing life as the "Hero's Journey," a cyclical process of challenge, transformation, and return. In every great story, the hero doesn't find peace after slaying the dragon or crossing the threshold. The journey continues. A new challenge emerges. Growth, Campbell argued, is not linear; it's cyclical. The quote, "The cave you fear to enter holds the treasure you seek." is famously attributed to him. While the exact wording is a paraphrase, it captures one of his core ideas: that what we fear most often hides the very growth we're seeking.

His sentiment is why I took on Ironman. I was an average swimmer and never liked cold water. But to finish an Ironman, I would have to swim 2.4 miles, 169 lengths of a pool, in about one hour and thirty minutes. To get to that level, I realized I would have to enter the cave Campbell described. After five years of swimming in the pool, in short races in cold water, and in the waves of the Chesapeake, I was ready. When I got out of the water in Tempe, Arizona, during my first Ironman, I nearly cried. My body was shaking from the cold, but inside, I felt something deeper: relief, pride, and exhilaration. I had entered the cave, and I had found the treasure. That's intentional living. There's no finish line—only the next cave to enter.

INTENTIONAL LIVING: A LIFELONG PRACTICE

Living with intention is not effortless.

It asks something of us—presence, honesty, choice.

In a world that rewards distraction and worships convenience, it's easier to numb than to notice.

Easier to scroll than to sit still.

Easier to move through the motions than to pause and ask,

"Is this the life I mean to live?"

It's easier to stay beneath the covers than to greet the morning with movement, with breath, with words.

But ease is not the goal…, meaning is.

And meaning is found in the quiet, deliberate moments we choose to show up.

Human history is rife with examples of this struggle. Our ancestors sought survival through routines and rituals that provided security and stability. In many ways, our brains are still wired for that same sense of homeostasis, a desire to stay safe and avoid change. By now, I am hopeful that we know that growth doesn't happen in comfort zones. It happens when we intentionally disrupt the status quo, challenge ourselves to do better, and commit to living in alignment with our highest values. Malcolm Gladwell, in *Outliers*, argues that mastery requires thousands of hours of deliberate practice.[3] The same applies to life. You can't wish yourself into intentional living; you must build it through repeated, deliberate effort. After riding my bike for over one hundred thousand miles, I remember telling my wife, "I finally know how to ride a bike." She looked at me like I was crazy, but I knew what I meant. Mastery isn't about technical skill; it's about embodiment. After thousands of hours, I wasn't just riding, I had become a rider. Like riding, intentional living becomes second nature, not because it's easy, but because it's ingrained. It's not about figuring it out intellectually; it's about living it until it becomes who we are. The more we choose intentionality over comfort, the easier it becomes. Small, consistent choices compound into a life of purpose and clarity.

WHY IS IT HARD TO DO WHAT'S GOOD FOR US?

People like to say, "We have met the enemy, and the enemy is us." We know what's good for us—exercise, eating well, building relationships, and meaningful work. But knowing and doing are two very different things. Why is it so hard to do what we know is right? The explanation, while simple, does not make it easy to fix. Essentially, we live in two states. One that craves growth, expansion, and meaning, and another that is fueled by fear, inertia, and comfort. The question is: What do we do with this conundrum? James Clear, in *Atomic Habits*, emphasizes small, consistent actions as the key to long-term success. He explains that it takes less energy to repeat the same behavior than to disrupt a habit and try something new.[4] Living intentionally builds on his approach and takes it a step further. It asks us to embrace discomfort, delay gratification, and commit to what truly matters, even when it's hard. Yes, it's easier to hit snooze than to get up early and exercise. It's easier to binge-watch a series than to read a book that challenges our thinking.

I have learned that we will never reach a point where it's effortless to make intentional choices. The pull of convenience and comfort will always be there. But with practice, we can strengthen our capacity to choose intentionally more often. We can even fall in love with the challenge, the hardship, and the discomfort, because even though we won't get instant gratification, we are building systems and habits that make intentionality the default. Over time, this compounds into real growth. And we can feel it; it is an energy that vibrates in us like no other, and it is incredibly fulfilling.

WHAT LIVING INTENTIONALLY HAS MEANT IN MY LIFE

Ryan Holiday, in *Stillness Is the Key*, reminds us that intentional living is not about constant movement, but about pausing and reflecting.

It's in the quiet moments that we gain clarity about our values, recognize our growth, and prepare for what's next. Without reflection, our lives become chaotic and unfocused.[5]

Throughout my life, I've learned that living intentionally isn't about grand gestures or radical transformations. It has been about teaching myself that small, consistent actions need to align with who I want to be. This led me to show up every day and choose to live with purpose, even when no one is watching. All my moments, my daily practices, and my C[3] culminated in everything I was able to do, like running six marathons on six continents in six days. It's meant starting businesses and projects that align with my values, even when the road was uncertain. It's meant writing a daily blog to reflect on my experiences and share insights with others. But most importantly, it's meant being present for the people I love. It's meant showing up for my family, my friends, and my community with grace, grit, and a commitment to making a positive impact. These moments, the ones where I choose to live intentionally in my relationships, my work, and my personal growth, are the moments that bring true fulfillment.

The good news is that there is no finish line. Life will always offer new peaks to climb and valleys to navigate. Just when you think you've reached the summit, another peak appears. The path shifts beneath your feet. And that's the point. Because in the infinite game, the goal isn't to win; it's to keep playing with purpose, to keep living intentionally, one present moment at a time. It's not about reaching a final destination; it's about continuing to evolve, to move forward, and to grow a little more each day.

David Goggins states, "You are in danger of living a life so comfortable and soft that you will die without ever realizing your true potential."[6]

Joseph Campbell tells us, "The very cave you are afraid to enter turns out to be the source of what you are looking for."[7]

Simon Sinek reminds us, "The goal is not to be perfect by the end. The goal is to be better today."[8]

Each voice points to the same truth: living intentionally isn't about arrival, it's about engagement. About leaning in, especially when it's hard.

So, the question isn't, "Have you arrived?"

The question is: "Are you still moving?"

Because the road never ends. And that's exactly the point.

CHAPTER 14

START NOW

This is the Moment

Are there limits? Do we need permission? Is life really that full? The clock is ticking. Our days are packed. And lost in the noise is what truly matters. The thing we really want to do. That dream. That shift. That change we keep putting off. We tell ourselves we're waiting for the right moment, the perfect conditions, the "sign." But the perfect moment is now. Life is already in motion. And the discomfort of beginning something new? It's nothing compared to the regret of never beginning at all. So, we must challenge ourselves to start. Not perfectly. Not with all the answers. Just honestly. Courageously. Now. Take the first step. Make the call. Apologize. Apply. Quit. Create. Say yes. Say no. Step up. Speak out. Slow down. Begin again. Whatever it is, this is the moment we permit ourselves to go. Because nothing changes until we do.

PLANT YOUR TREE

I love the saying, "The best time to plant a tree was twenty years ago. The second-best time is today." But let's be clear—intentional living isn't about regretting the tree you didn't plant. It's about choosing to plant it now. The well-worn path toward intentional living doesn't require a grand plan or perfect circumstances. It simply requires a decision, a decision to begin. Not tomorrow, not next week, not when life gets easier. Today. We don't know how much time we have. The only moment we have control over is the one we're in right now. So why wait? Why put off living the life you want to live? Why delay becoming the person you want to be?

When people ask if there was a moment when I felt the switch from a conventional, achievement-driven life to one rooted in intentionality, I remember it vividly. In many ways, that moment is why I believe we all have a path to living intentionally. I thought I had done everything "right." I listened to everyone: work hard, make money, get promoted, play the game. And I did it; promotions, raises, bonuses, everything I believed would make me happy was right there. Yet, I felt empty. Results-oriented. Soulless. I had become a one-dimensional actor in the play of life. Excellent, but not extraordinary. Successful, but not fulfilled. It struck me: I wasn't living. I was performing. And success had become the trap.

This can't be it, I thought. *There must be more.*

That's when I decided to break free. It started small: a push-up, a single mile on the road, a bold choice to walk away from a lot of money led me to leave the corporate machine for a smaller company. I didn't have a grand plan, just a deep, persistent urge to reclaim my life. I didn't know where it would lead; I only knew I couldn't stay where I was. Slowly, step by step, I began to rebuild from the inside out. I started thinking differently about purpose, commitment, account-ability, and what it truly meant to live intentionally. Over time, some-thing powerful began to take shape: a force pushing me forward and away from everything I used to chase. I didn't know where it would lead, but I just knew I couldn't remain where I was. And for sure, I could never have imagined that, years later, I would find myself writ-ing a book called *Living Intentionally*, but that's how the path always begins: one step, one choice, one intention.

START SMALL. START NOW

You don't need to figure it all out. You don't need a perfect plan. You just need to start. Before you close this book, take a moment for your-self. Reflect. Get honest. Here's how to begin:

Step 1: Write down one small intention you can commit to today.

Step 2: Ask yourself: "Does this align with the person I want to become?"

Step 3: Make it easy to succeed. Keep it small and specific, like a five-minute walk each morning, reaching out to someone you care about, putting your phone away at dinner, or reading a page from a book instead of scrolling a newsfeed. It doesn't have to be big. It just needs to be intentional.

CREATING THE WORLD WE WANT TO LIVE IN

Imagine a world where more people choose to live intentionally. Where individuals prioritize connection, compassion, and contribution.

Where communities are built on shared values and mutual support. What would be possible if more people committed to living beyond themselves? If, in every interaction, individuals chose understanding over judgment, curiosity over complacency, and compassion over indifference. A world where we each prioritized service over self-interest and sought ways to lift each other up, not compete for attention or recognition.

Living intentionally isn't about perfection; it's about courage. It means choosing discomfort over ease, purpose over passivity, and growth over stagnation. It means showing up, even when we don't feel ready. *Especially* when we don't feel ready. Living intentionally isn't a burden; it's a gift. It's an invitation to continually evolve, grow, and make a meaningful impact on the world around us.

We are standing at the edge.

On one side: the life we've always known.

On the other: the life we were meant to live.

Living with purpose, grit, and grace is more than a personal choice; it's a collective movement. One that can reshape the fabric of our communities and create a future where we all share in the abundance around us, defined by peak performance, empathy, mutual respect, and shared values. Because the collective effect of all of us living intentionally is immeasurable.

Yes, it is ok to start small. But start now. Time is shorter than you think. Because once you do, something shifts. A spark catches. The first action leads to the second. The discomfort becomes fuel. The ordinary moment becomes sacred when we show up for it fully, with intention and heart. This is how you change your life. Not with a single massive act, but through thousands of intentional moments. Showing up when it would be easier to check out. Saying "yes" to what matters. Saying "no" to what doesn't. Being present. Choosing courage over comfort. Integrity over convenience. Purpose over drifting.

Start the thing that's been whispering to you.

Start the habit that aligns with who you want to become.

Start showing up as the version of you that no longer settles.

Because the world needs more people who are fully alive.

And that, more than anything, is what living intentionally is about, not perfection, not status, not comparison. It's about waking up each day and choosing to live with depth, with meaning, and with heart. And while this book ends here, your real story begins now. There's no perfect moment. No better time.

So, take a deep breath—and start now.

Your intentional journey begins.

Because the life you want isn't waiting.

THE NEXT CHAPTER IS YOURS

You made it to the final page, but this isn't the end. This is the invitation. The turning point. The quiet, powerful moment where you decide what happens next. Because everything you need to begin living intentionally is already within you. The grit to keep going. The grace to forgive. The groundedness to stay true. The awareness to choose your next move on purpose. This is about looking in the mirror and loving who we see. It's about being present. It's not about fixing your life. It's about owning it. The practices, reflections, and stories in this book are not a prescription; they're a framework. A guide. A reminder that your life is not something that happens to you; it's something you create, shape, and reimagine every single day.

So, what will you do with your one wild and precious life?

Will you push your limits?

Will you step into discomfort?

Will you reach out, stand up, slow down, and go deeper?

The next chapter of your life hasn't been written. The pen is in your hand.

Live it boldly. Live it fully.

Live it intentionally.

ACKNOWLEDGMENTS

It has been quite a few years since I wrote *Living the High Performance Life*, and for sure, a lot of life has been lived since then. I have kept up my daily writing, but for all my attempts, I just did not get book number two going. I knew there was something in me that needed to be written, but as life often reminds us, we all need a little nudge or support to take on an effort such as writing a book. A call with my dear friend, Anca, was the catalyst. She said I needed to write this book, and now I know why. I will forever be grateful for her push. *Living Intentionally* is the culmination of my experiences, but even more so, the wisdom, encouragement, and lessons I have gained from so many along the way. This book needed to be written.

First, to my family, you have allowed me to be me, which I know sometimes, or all the time, can be a bit much. You have learned to tolerate my uncompromising nature when I get a goal in my head, and I will never be able to thank you enough for your support. It bears saying that your unwavering love and belief in me have been the foundation of everything I do.

To Anthea, your support, love, patience, and encouragement have been my steady foundation, allowing me the space to dream and create. I have been able to count on you being in my corner for the past thirty-plus years, and you are truly my rock. It seems impossible to thank you enough.

To Julianne and Kimberly, I am so grateful to be your dad and to go on this journey together. Thank you for caring for me, supporting me, teaching me, and reminding me every day what it means to live fully and love deeply.

Dad and Mom, thank you for the love and support, for the best family life anyone could ever have, for pushing me to be better, and for loving me even in my most ridiculous moments. When I am asked how I became the way I am, I smile, knowing that you both are the secret ingredient. I am forever thankful for both of you! Love you!

Beth, you have been my biggest fan, and I admire not just who you are, but the way you show up for everyone, always, without hesitation. I could not have a better sister.

Ted, thanks for letting me chase you on the tennis court, around the golf course, and on the bike. It made me better.

To my friends like Joe D., and my community on all platforms, you have embraced who I am and appreciate the path that I have chosen. I just hope that I have lived up to what you want from your friend and colleague. Thanks for listening to my endless stories and for encouraging me to tell more.

To the authors, podcasters, thinkers, and leaders whose work has shaped my philosophy, thank you for pushing the boundaries of thought and daring to ask the hard questions. Your insights have been invaluable in shaping the ideas within this book.

To my editor, Robert, you helped me take this book to the next level. I love your eye for detail and how you pushed me to tell more stories. Thank you for believing in this project and ensuring that its message is as strong and clear as possible.

Finally, to you, the reader, thank you for being here, for seeking growth, and for choosing to live with intention. This book is for you. The road you're on is uniquely yours, and I hope these pages serve as a guide, a challenge, and an invitation to step into your fullest potential. The world needs more people like you. Keep going. Keep pushing. The pursuit of intentional living never ends.

With gratitude,

Joe

NOTES

CHAPTER 1: DEFINING OUR *WHY*

1. Maria Konnikova, *Mastermind: How to Think Like Sherlock Holmes* (Canongate, 2013), 779, Internet Archive.

2. Michael F. Steger, et al. "The Meaning in Life Questionnaire: Assessing the Presence of and Search for Meaning in Life," *Journal of Counseling Psychology*, 53, no. 1 (2006): 80–93, https://doi.org/10.1037/0022-0167.53.1.80.

3. Rich Roll, host, *The Rich Roll Podcast*, episode 889, "Fasting for Longevity: Valter Longo, PhD Shares Cutting-Edge Fasting Science & Optimal Nutrition Protocols for Lifespan Extension & Disease Prevention," Apple Podcasts, February 10, 2025, 2:04:08, https://podcasts.apple.com/us/podcast/fasting-for-longevity-valter-longo-phd-shares-cutting/id582272991?i=1000690794448.

4. Malala Yousafzai with Christina Lamb, *I Am Malala: The Girl Who Stood Up for Education and was Shot by the Taliban* (Weidenfeld & Nicolson, 2013), Internet Archive.

5. Alfred Lansing, *Endurance: Shackleton's Incredible Voyage* (Basic Books, 2014).

CHAPTER 2: BUILDING OUR PILLARS

1. Angela Duckworth, *Grit: The Power of Passion and Perseverance* (Scribner, 2018).

2. Brené Brown, *The Gifts of Imperfection: Let Go of Who You Think You're Supposed to Be and Embrace Who You Are* (Hazelden Publishing, 2010), Internet Archive; *Daring Greatly: How the Courage to Be Vulnerable Transforms the Way We Live, Love, Parent, and Lead* (Gotham Books, 2012), IEEE Web Hosting.

3. Roger Federer, "2024 Commencement Address by Roger Federer at Dartmouth," speech, June 9, 2024, posted by Dartmouth, YouTube, 25:03, https://www.youtube.com/watch?v=pqWUuYTcG-o.

4. Maxwell King, *The Good Neighbor: The Life and Work of Fred Rogers* (Abrams Press, 2018), Dokumen.

5. Juliet Macur, "Simone Biles is Withdrawing from the Olympics All-Around Gymnastics Competition," *New York Times*, July 28, 2021, https://www.nytimes.com/2021/07/28/sports/olympics/simone-biles-out.html.

6. James Clear, *Atomic Habits* (Avery, 2018).

7. Clear, *Atomic Habits*, chapter 2.

8. Ryan Holiday, *The Daily Stoic: 366 Meditations on Wisdom, Perseverance, and the Art of Living* (Portfolio, 2016).

CHAPTER 3: EMBRACE THE CHALLENGE

1. Marcus Aurelius, *Meditations*, trans. Gregory Hays (Modern Library, 2002), book 5, Internet Archive, https://archive.org/details/meditation-GeorgeHays/page/n305/mode/2up?q=%22what+stands+in+the+way+becomes%22.

2. Michael Easter, *The Comfort Crisis: Embrace Discomfort to Reclaim Your Wild, Happy, Healthy Self* (Rodale Books, 2021), chapter 1.

3. Christopher Bergland, "Low-to-Moderate Doses of Stress May Fortify Resilience," *Psychology Today*, May 21, 2024, https://www.psychologytoday.com/us/blog/the-athletes-way/202208/low-to-moderate-doses-of-stress-may-fortify-resilience.

4. Rich Roll, host, *The Rich Roll Podcast*, episode 887, "Win the Inside Game: High Performance Psychology, Busting Fitness Myths, & Getting Unstuck With Elite Coach Steve Magness," Apple Podcasts, January 30, 2025, 2:21:28, https://podcasts.apple.com/au/podcast/win-the-inside-game-high-performance-psychology/id582272991?i=1000687083644.

5. Erno J. Hermans, et al., "Building Resilience: The Stress Response as a Driving Force for Neuroplasticity and Adaptation," *Biological Psychiatry* 94, no. 4 (2024): 330-338, https://doi.org/10.1016/j.biopsych.2024.10.016.

6. Diana Nyad, *Find a Way* (Vintage, 2016).

7. Mel Robbins, *The 5 Second Rule: Transform Your Life, Work, and Confidence with Everyday Courage* (Savio Republic, 2017), chapter 4.

CHAPTER 4: MASTERING REFLECTION

1. Plato, "Apology," trans. G. M. A. Grube, in *Plato: Complete Works*, ed. John M. Cooper and D. S. Hutchinson (Hackett Publishing Company, 1997), Internet Archive.

2. Marcus Aurelius, *Meditations*, trans. Gregory Hays (Modern Library, 2003), Internet Archive, https://archive.org/details/meditation-GeorgeHays/page/n305/mode/2up?q=%22what+stands+in+the+way+becomes%22.

3. Melanie Perkins, "Canva CEO Melanie Perkins on Turning Mistakes into Lessons," June 21, 2019, https://thriveglobal.com/articles/canva-ceo-melanie-perkins-on-turning-mistakes-into-lessons.

4. Gretchen Rubin, *The Happiness Project* (Harper, 2011).

5. Kelly Berry, host, *Life Intended*, season 1, episode 35, "10 Questions for a More Intentional Life," Apple Podcasts, November 19, 2024, 29 min., 31 sec., https://podcasts.apple.com/us/podcast/solo-episode-10-questions-for-a-more-intentional-life/id1742338888?i=1000677452199.

6. Ray Dalio, *Principles: Life and Work* (Avid Reader Press/Simon & Schuster, 2017).

7. Giada Di Stefano, et al., "Learning by Thinking: How Reflection Aids Performance," Harvard Business School NOM Unit Working Paper No. 14-093 (2014): 1-36, http://dx.doi.org/10.2139/ssrn.2414478.

8. Marcus E. Raichle, "The Brain's Default Mode Network," *Annual Review of Neuroscience* 38 (2015): 433–447, https://doi.org/10.1146/annurev-neuro-071013-014030.

9. Francesca Gino and Gary P. Pisano, "Why Leaders Don't Learn From Success," *Harvard Business Review*, April 2011, https://hbr.org/2011/04/why-leaders-dont-learn-from-success.

CHAPTER 5: FROM FAILURE TO FUEL

1. Steven Bartlett, host, *The Diary of a CEO with Steven Bartlett*, "The Manipulation Expert: Most People Don't Realise They're Narcissists! You're Setting Your Child Up for Misery," Apple Podcasts, February 26, 2025, 2:44:14, https://podcasts.apple.com/bs/podcast/the-manipulation-expert -most-people-dont-realise/id1291423644?i=1000696464492.

2. Adam Grant, host, *WorkLife with Adam Grant*, "The Art of Failure with David Ducho-vny," Apple Podcasts, May 7, 2024, 37 min., 13 sec., https://podcasts.apple.com/us/podcast/ the-art-of-failure-with-david-duchovny/id1346314086?i=1000654720827.

3. Irvin D. Yalom, *Staring at the Sun: Overcoming the Terror of Death* (Jossey-Bass, 2008), 92, ResearchGate.

4. Tony Robbins, host, *The Tony Robbins Podcast*, "Start Small, Think Big, Scale Quickly | SPANX Founder Sarah Blakely on how to Bootstrap a Billion Dollar Business," Apple Podcasts, March 9, 2020, 1:15:59, https://podcasts.apple.com/us/podcast/start-small-think-big-scale-quickly -spanx-founder-sara/id1098413063?i=1000467901109.

5. Tim Newman, "Exercise Prevents Cellular Aging by Boosting Mitochondria," *Medical News Today*, March 8, 2017, https://www.medicalnewstoday.com/articles/316229.

CHAPTER 6: GO BIG OR GO HOME

1. James Clear, *Atomic Habits* (Avery, 2018).

CHAPTER 7: FINDING MEANING THROUGH SUFFERING

1. Kylie Kelce, host, *Not Gonna Lie*, season 1, episode 4, "Kylie on Inevitable Minivan Future, Online Clapbacks & Body Neutrality with Drew Afualo," Apple Podcasts, January 2, 2025, 44 min., 50 sec., https://podcasts.apple.com/us/podcast/kylie-on-inevitable-minivan-future-online-clapbacks/ id1780888125?i=1000682394613.

2. Ryan Holiday, *The Obstacle Is the Way: The Timeless Art of Turning Trials into Triumph* (Portfo-lio, 2014).

3. Marcus Aurelius, *Meditations*, trans. Gregory Hays (Modern Library, 2003), Internet Archive, https://archive.org/details/meditation-GeorgeHays/page/n305/mode/2up?q=%22what+stand s+in+the+way+becomes%22.

4. Holiday, *The Obstacle Is the Way*.

5. "Daily Time Spent Streaming Netflix per Account Worldwide in 1st Half 2023 and 2nd Half 2024" Statista, published March 5, 2025 https://www.statista.com/statistics/1497100/ time-spent-streaming-netflix-per-account/.

6. Liese Exelmans and Jan Van den Bulck, "Binge Viewing, Sleep, and the Role of Pre-Sleep Arousal," *Journal of Clinical Sleep Medicine* 13, no. 8 (2017): 1001-08, https://doi.org/10.5664/ jcsm.6704.

7. Kat Edwards Anderson, "As Iron Sharpens Iron // A Moab 240 Story" posted March 7, 2025, by Jason + Kat, YouTube, 23:50, https://www.youtube.com/watch?v=7M6re00m4as.

8. Viktor E. Frankl, *Man's Search for Meaning* (Beacon Press, 2006).

CHAPTER 8: THE POWER OF CONNECTION

1. Robert Waldinger and Marc Schulz, *The Good Life: Lessons from the World's Longest Scientific Study of Happiness* (Simon & Schuster, 2023), Dokumen.

2. Warren Bennis and Patricia Ward Biederman, *Organizing Genius* (Basic Books, 1998).

3. Eva Ritvo M.D., "The Neuroscience of Giving," *Psychology Today*, April 24, 2014, https://www.psychologytoday.com/us/blog/vitality/201404/the-neuroscience-giving.

CHAPTER 9: BE PRESENT EVERY DAY

1. *Ageless Living: The Secret of Happiness and Longevity*, season 1, episode 24, "Living the High Performance Life Part 2," directed by George Cappannelli, featuring Joe Gagnon, aired May 1, 2020, on PBS.

2. Ellen J. Langer, *Mindfulness* (Da Capo Press, 1989), Internet Archive, https://archive.org/details/mindfulness0000lang/page/n7/mode/2up.

3. Mihaly Csikszentmihalyi, *Flow: The Psychology of Optimal Experience* (Harper Perennial, 1991), Internet Archive, https://archive.org/details/flow-the-psychology-of-optimal-experience-pdfdrive/page/n3/mode/2up.

4. Steven Kotler, *The Art of Impossible: A Peak Performance Primer* (Harper, 2023).

5. Steven Kotler, *The Rise of Superman: Decoding the Science of Ultimate Human Performance* (Quercus Publishing, 2014); Steven Kotler and Jamie Wheal, *Stealing Fire* (Dey Street Books, 2018).

CHAPTER 11: BUILDING OUR PERSONAL HEALTH PLATFORM

1. Tim Newman, "Exercise Prevents Cellular Aging by Boosting Mitochondria," *Medical News Today*, March 8, 2017, https://www.medicalnewstoday.com/articles/316229.

2. Kristin L. Szuhany, Matteo Bugatti, and Michael W. Otto, "A Meta-Analytic Review of the Effects of Exercise on Brain-Derived Neurotropic Factor," *Journal of Psychiatric Research* 60 (2015): 56-64, https://doi.org/10.1016/j.jpsychires.2014.10.003.

3. "Physical Activity Boosts Brain Health," Center for Disease Control, posted January 21, 2025, https://www.cdc.gov/physical-activity/features/boost-brain-health.html.

4. Kassandra Kaleda, "Exercise and Hormones: Understanding the Balancing Act," The Nutrition Institute, published April 16, 2025, https://www.thenutritioninstitute.com/au/en/blog-exercise-and-hormones.

5. Peter Attia, host, *The Peter Attia Drive*, episode 261, "Training for The Centenarian Decathlon: Zone 2, VO2 Max, Stability, and Strength," Apple Podcasts, July 10, 2023, 1:04:50, https://podcasts.apple.com/us/podcast/training-for-the-centenarian-decathlon-zone-2-vo2-max/id1400828889?i=1000620484439.

6. Peter Attia, *Outlive: The Science & Art of Longevity* (Harmony, 2023), Chapter 1.

7. "Obesity and Overweight," Center for Disease Control, last reviewed October 25, 2024, https://www.cdc.gov/nchs/fastats/obesity-overweight.htm.

8. Kevin D. Hall et al., "Ultra-Processed Diets Cause Excess Calorie Intake and Weight Gain: An Inpatient Randomized Controlled Trial of Ad Libitum Food Intake," *Cell Metabolism* 30, no.

1 (2019): 67–77.e3, https://doi10.1016/j.cmet.2019.05.008; Carlos A. Monteiro et al., "Ultra-Processed Foods: What They Are and How to Identify Them," *Public Health Nutrition* 22, no. 5 (2019): 936–941, https:// 10.1017/S1368980018003762.

9. Monica Reinagel, host, *Nutrition Diva*, https://podcasts.apple.com/us/podcast/nutrition-diva/id289338154.

10. "Food Availability (Per Capita) Data System," U.S. Department of Agriculture, last updated January 8, 2025, https://www.ers.usda.gov/data-products/food-availability-per-capita-data-system.

11. U.S. Environmental Protection Agency, *Report to Congress on Indoor Air Quality: Volume 2* (EPA, 1989), EPA/400/1-89/001C.

12. Matthew Walker, *Why We Sleep: Unlocking the Power of Sleep and Dreams* (Scribner, 2017), chapter 1, Internet Archive.

13. Andrew Huberman, host, *Huberman Lab Podcast*, https://podcasts.apple.com/us/podcast/huberman-lab/id1545953110.

14. Carol Dweck, *Mindset: The New Psychology of Success* (Ballantine Books, 2013).

15. Rich Roll and Julie Platt, *The Plantpower Way: Whole Food Plant-Based Recipes and Guidance for the Whole Family* (Avery, 2015), 152.

16. Robert Waldinger, "What Makes a Good Life? Lessons From the Longest Study on Happiness," TED Talk, November 2015, 12 min., 37 sec., https://www.ted.com/talks/robert_waldinger _what_makes_a_good_life_lessons_from_the_longest_study_on_happiness.

17. Dan Buettner, *The Blue Zones: Lessons for Living Longer from the People Who've Lived the Longest* (National Geographic, 2008).

18. Attia, *Outlive*.

CHAPTER 12: LIVING BEYOND OURSELVES

1. James Clear, *Atomic Habits* (Avery, 2018), 35.

2. Angela Duckworth, *Grit: The Power of Passion and Perseverance* (Scribner, 2018).

3. Viktor E. Frankl, *Man's Search for Meaning* (Beacon Press, 2006).

4. Fred Rogers, *The World According to Mister Rogers: Important Things to Remember* (Hyperion, 2003), 81, Internet Archive, https://archive.org/details/worldaccordingto00roge.

5. Simon Sinek, *The Infinite Game* (Portfolio Penguin, 2019).

6. Steven Bartlett, host, *The Diary of a CEO with Steven Bartlett*, "Simon Sinek: Opens Up About His Struggle with Loneliness, Love, and Dating," Apple Podcasts, March 16, 2023, 1:57:44, https://podcasts.apple.com/us/podcast/simon-sinek-opens-up-about-his-struggle-with/id1291423644?i=1000604444064.

CHAPTER 13: THE ENDLESS JOURNEY

1. Simon Sinek, *The Infinite Game* (Portfolio Penguin, 2019).

2. David Goggins, *Can't Hurt Me: Master Your Mind and Defy the Odds* (Lioncrest Publishing, 2018), 211.

3. Malcolm Gladwell, *Outliers: The Story of Success* (Little, Brown and Company, 2008), chapter 2.

4. James Clear, *Atomic Habits* (Avery, 2018).

5. Ryan Holiday, *Stillness Is the Key* (Portfolio, 2019).

6. David Goggins, *Can't Hurt Me*, 10.

7. Joseph Campbell, *A Joseph Campbell Companion: Reflections on the Art of Living*, ed. Diane K. Osbon (HarperPerennial, 1995), 24, Internet Archive, https://archive.org/details/josephcampbellco0000camp/page/n5/mode/2up.

8. Simon Sinek (@simonsinek), "The goal is not to be perfect by the end. The goal is to be better today.," Twitter (Now X), October 13, 2020, https://x.com/simonsinek/status/1316054597 232975875?lang=en.

ABOUT THE AUTHOR

Joe Gagnon - *Relentlessly Intentional | CEO | Ultra-Endurance Athlete | Coach | Author | Obsessed with Unlocking Human Potential*

Joe Gagnon is driven by a simple mission: helping people realize they are capable of far more than they think is possible. Over the years, he has led six companies as CEO, coached elite performers, and pushed himself to physical and mental extremes: completing six Ironman races, running hundred-mile ultramarathons, and finishing six marathons on six continents in six days.

As CEO of Raynmaker, he is building an AI-powered sales platform designed to help small businesses grow smarter and faster. As a high-performance coach, he partners with bold, ambitious leaders to break through self-imposed limits and lead lives of deeper purpose and greater impact.

Joe's life and this book are rooted in the belief that growth happens on the edge. It's in the uncomfortable, uncertain, and transformational moments that we discover who we really are. Every step he takes is guided by the principles of grit, grace, and groundedness. Whether he's building a company, mentoring a founder, or speaking on stage, his goal remains the same: to inspire others to live intentionally by design, not by default.

FOLLOW JOE ON THE FOLLOWING WEBSITES:

www.linkedin.com/in/joegagnon/

substack.com/@joecurious

www.thehighperformancelife.net/

www.instagram.com/thehighperformancelife